THE OWL MOON LAB

A PARANORMAL EXPERIMENT

TOBE JOHNSON

HANGAR 1 PUBLISHING

CONTENTS

FOREWORD

My strange and unusual story started in December 2017 when I moved from Glide, Oregon, to the Owl Moon Lab House near Cottage Grove, Oregon. At night, almost immediately after moving into the new residence, we began hearing strange and unusual sounds coming from the thick forest directly behind our property. As an avid hunter, those sounds were like nothing I had ever heard. We attempted to begin recording them, however, it was December, cold, and pouring down with rain, making it hard to record anything. In addition, upon moving in, we also began hearing noises inside the home.

Shortly after moving into the residence, we built from scratch a large metal shop building. Upon completion, strange things began to happen within. Items, tools, and other things were being moved from one location to another. On top of all of that, there were a lot of deafening noises coming from inside. Additionally, there were unknown male and female voices that we were able to catch through recording.

As the season changed into Spring and the weather was much nicer, the noises, voices, banging, and overall activity steadily increased. We heard more screams, howls, whoops, and countless other noises from the forest, which we also recorded using our parabolic recording equipment. We began noticing little trinkets, some would call gifts, showing up around the property. Many of the gifts, most amazingly, seemed to be connected to our own private conversations we had while relaxing at home. For instance, one conversation between my wife and me was about the heart surgery she had years previous. The next day or two later, my wife found a pink glass heart that fit in the palm of her hand. It was placed in a tree she was trimming. Many have said that this home could easily change a person's thinking. This is why I coined the phrase, "I was normal when I got here."

Darrell Adams

QR EXPERIENCE INSTRUCTIONS

To operate the QR codes within the pages, simply point any smartphone at the QR code square like you are going to take a photo. Your phone should immediately prompt you to the link needed to access the Owl Moon Lab audio, video, and photos. Click that link. Headphones or earbuds are suggested for an optimal audio experience.

1

IN THE BEGINNING

Before we begin, this is not a story for those seeking answers to questions they think they already know. This is a story about questions that ask harder questions. For me, it started in the forest and ends in the forest. It's in the shadows of giant Doug Firs and Sword Fern-lined trails where a simple question was asked, "What goes around the bend?"

When I was a child in Pleasant Hill, Oregon, home to such things as berry fields, Ken Kesey's estate and broken down Chevy's, I recall a certain midnight showing my father let me stay up to watch. It was the story of a witness who could not let go. I now know the movie to be Close Encounters of the Third Kind. The quote Richard Dreyfuss's character (Roy Neary) repeats is a mantra, "THIS MEANS SOMETHING!" That was the quote that carried me through my adolescence into my teenage years and adulthood.

I was, and still am set apart from others, based upon this question, "What goes around the bend?" Where excepted science left off, that for me is where the real adventure begins.

Without belaboring all the details of growing up as an only child with a single mother in the small broken downtown of Springfield, Oregon, yes Bart Simpson's home, I can tell you my years have been blessed. I have become a father to a young man that defines my role as Proud Dad. I have loved and lost, but who hasn't? I have set sail on the seven seas as Navy Corpsman and chosen every job available after, from driving a semi-truck, shooting x-rays, a hospice in a haunted house; now that was an interesting 4 weeks. I am what you call a vagabond and moss don't gather easily on the Johnson men. My father, who I only know the darker side of, is like this as well, a mover and gypsy.

So now you know enough for us to begin, you have your template of a personality somewhat and the rest is up to the imagination.

Our story cannot begin without getting a couple of things out of the way. First, this is not just a Sasquatch story, it is the true account of how Sasquatch led me deeper. By that I mean, in searching for a mere physical sighting, I came to know more about me and my fellow man. I came to know how small I was and how deep the infinite unknown is. Sasquatch is a foundation to build off, it sets typically "a young man's imagination afire" with adventure in the wild and the hopes of being transformed. This is the true nature of Sasquatch. For me, this transformation happened over a period of 15 years and brought me to a small property in Cottage Grove, Oregon. It was at this property the Owl Moon Lab came to be.

Before we begin, we must chronologically go through specific dates of my inquiry into the world of Sasquatch. I should tell you, upon initially looking into this subject I was in a liminal state between 2 worlds, growing from one relationship to another. I suppose if I was transparent, I saw Sasquatch as a way to deal with deep depression. Well, I took to it like a drug and sought conventions, eyewitness testimony, and areas of recent sightings. However, my main focus was what I now call EESI's translation - Extended Experiencers of Sasquatch Interaction. It's in seeking people that I found some of us had Sasquatch in our backyard. A detail that will be hard for some to believe, but you ain't heard nothing yet. So, with that...let us start four years after my son was born in the mill town of Thurston, Oregon. It's in Thurston I began to not only question, this means something, but...this means something else.

Dec.2007
LIMINAL

I was recently divorced and shared dual custody of my only son. However, my ex-wife and I still communicated about activities to share with our child. One pastime would stand out more than others as we both still shared the joy of hiking. So on a particularly cold December day, we both met up with my Son in tow at a mutual and close two-hour hiking spot. I hugged my boy and waved presumptively to my ex as she grabbed a sack lunch. The three of us double-knotted our laces and began the hike over the suburban hillside. The area was known for nicer homes set up above Thurston. It was a locals hangout known not only for hiking and dog walking but also truancy. My hometown high school was down at the bottom of the suburban hillside and the trails we were on would get the occasional seventeen-year-old flunkey who would nest up in the crook of a tree and load their bong. It was the perfect spot ya wanna build a pallet boarded treehouse and flip through Smuthouse magazine. Although I never found myself with that rebellion, I understood the draw of being defiant and going off the radar.

As we walked up the path, the early morning air was crisp and wet. The ice melted slowly in the wet mud, and the clear blue morning sky only dropped the temperature. We hiked up through the southern shadow of the Thurston Cliffs. My son walked ahead and I followed behind with my ex. After about fifteen minutes of our slow ascent, we stopped near a bend in the trail where my son was pointing down at something. He piped, "Dad, is that a Sasquatch track?" I said, "Well that would be awesome, ya think ya see something?"

INITIAL TRACK

I walked up to where he stood and noticed what he was pointing at. It showed attributes of a bare-footed impression in the frozen trail. It showed 5 toes, a heel, and the exterior and interior of a single-footed size 11-inch human-type track. I explained that bears can leave a double step track, but this looked different. I then mentioned the high-schoolers who were up here with us on winter break, and that this would be the perfect place for a hoax. Perhaps they were here even now, waiting for someone to happen by so that they could record the whole moment for a quick laugh. I said, "Well ya know son, it looks pretty good just the same. I think we should take a photo of it and stick a scale object in the frame." Sticking a small scale object such as a dollar bill or envelope, or in my case, a red hiking whistle, gives size to just how large the track is. So, quickly and with little thought, we took a quick smartphone photo! The one curious thing about the track was that it was deep for such a compacted area in the frozen ground, and it looked fairly fresh as it was heading into the blackberry bushes.

About 3 months later nothing much had become of the photo on my phone, but it erupted a curiosity in me I was sharing with my son. Divorce sucks. No matter how happy you are to be leaving your ex, the triage work that needs to be done with kids is painful. I never wanted to be a statistic with marriage so maybe that's part of the reason I clung so quick to feed my son's new curiosity. I decided that the photo was good enough, that I could approach someone who knew better about these things. Luckily, we had someone in mind, and he had more than a better idea about Sasquatch.

Ron Olson was someone in the world of Sasquatch. He was at one time a well-known producer and business mogul who invested time and money into the phenomena. He financed the 1970s classic movie, SASQUATCH: The Legend of Bigfoot, filmed near the Three Sisters Wilderness. Ron was more than just a curious filmmaker, he sought out the legend full time and even had his Sasquatch shrine to the subject in one of his Eugene offices. He's said to have been on friendly terms with Roger Patters and Bob Gimlin during his hay-day and the movie he produced shares a common theme of trackers on horseback that comes face to face with the mystery.

After a couple of informal phone calls to Olson, he suggested I speak to a river guide named Dan Rogers. Apparently, this guy had active Sasquatch research spots and may be willing to talk to me about his experiences. I was warned by Olson that the guy "is a little bit out there." I took that with a grain of salt and thought, well...you would have to be a "little out there," and it was not a put down in my book.

2008
ROGERS WARNING

Dan Rogers was an interesting fella who was what I would call an anxious and reluctant witness. When we first met, we decided it best to meet at a public park and have a cup of coffee. I sat down, eager to hear the details of what he saw. His details surrounding the events of each encounter were very specific but almost too incredible. He was describing seeing multiple Sasquatch over his years of being an outdoorsman. He described coming as close as 20 feet from one between him and his truck. His stories ranged from fantasy to possible delusion, perhaps symptomatic of a lonely man who needed wonder and meaning. I listened all the same but overall I was overwhelmed with contempt for him wasting my time. Then he said something that caught my attention. At the very end of our initial meeting, as I was walking back to my car, Rogers said, "I'd tell ya the rest of the story, but it's far too weird and you would never believe me." I turned back to him and said, "Let's meet up next weekend, I want to know the rest of the story." There was something about him adding that final comment that told me I was being way too quick to judge from my initial interaction with a stranger. So, we met, and Rogers told me the rest of the story and he was correct, it was far too weird, however, I did believe him. Something told me this was information I would need later.

After a couple of months emailing, we set out a couple of dates to try for a campout, as the snow was melting from the Oregon Cascades. Rogers believed we would stand a good shot at getting into the backcountry before anyone else. So on a cold Nov. 2009, we drove in his truck for an overnight up near a spot called Cougar Lake. The snow was still falling as we hit 2500 ft. and Rogers decided that we were now in danger of getting stuck in the snow if we went any higher. We pulled over and grabbed the tailgate for the rest of the night. No fire, no noise, just the sound of wind and small bits of ice rain pecking down on the roof.

I broke the silence by whispering to Rogers, just what did he mean by the "story being far too weird?" For the rest of the night, between shivering to death, Rogers laid out his entire story.

He described how Sasquatch can follow you home from hundreds of miles away. Rogers described how they can control animals in the forest and use them as a distraction or a weapon. He alluded to them reading your mind or talking to you telepathically. He said they can turn invisible, walk right up to you and blow in your face. These were all extraordinary claims without a thread of proof, but he told me all this without caring what I thought. He must have assumed any guy who's willing to drive out here and sleep in the snow with someone he barely knows may be worth telling the rest of the story.

The last time we met he told me something that stayed with me and haunts me today. He said, "They can suck you into their world and before you know it, thirty years of chasing shadows will have replaced your own life for theirs."

2010
BIGFOOT & BEER

The hook was set after meeting Rogers and although his warning wandered around in the back of my head, I was set on meeting more witnesses and learning what they knew. They couldn't all have stories like his. There had to be a wide variety of encounter types and I wanted to know them all. I felt behind the curve of the phenomena and needed a place to learn and speak with witnesses more often. It would just so happen that after following up on a recent Sasquatch sighting area, I would stop in at a place called Ike's Pizza in Leaburg, Oregon. I walked in and saw a newspaper article from California that said, "Local man sees Sasquatch." I asked who appeared to be the owner of the restaurant if he knew the fella the article was talking about? He said, "You betcha, I do, it's my cook back there." I ended up staying for hours talking back and forth to the cook who had little else to do in the empty restaurant than relate his incredible Sasquatch encounter.

A couple of weeks later I went back to Ike's and approached the owner with the concept of a live show called Bigfoot & Beer. The idea was simple, I would pack the house once a month with locals who wanted to hear a good Sasquatch encounter story, and in return, Ike's would get the dinner crowd to order family-style portions for a profit. They had nothing to lose by trying something different to bring in customers, so a deal was struck.

At first, the structure of witness testimony over dinner was done on the fly. We mostly set up witnesses to talk to twenty people or less while they ordered a pitcher of beer and a large pizza pie. However, word got out quickly and in a couple of months, the newspaper wrote an article that boosted our audience/customer count. Twenty turned to forty, and then eventually came local and national media.

One of the first witnesses I remember relating his encounter story was a lawyer by the name of Jeff Boiler. He had only lived a couple of miles away from the restaurant and must have seen a flyer we had hanging out of the window. Boiler approached me in private and it was obvious he was excited to relate the story of his encounter to

someone who believed him. I listened intently and watched him relive
the whole experience. He said in the 1980's he was hiking in the Three
Sisters Wilderness visiting a spot where his deceased friend's ashes
were spread. He wanted to revisit and pay homage to the anniversary
of his passing. It was on that solo hike that he saw something red shift
its way on the bluff up ahead. As he approached what he assumed was
the backside of an elk, he soon realized he was in fact face to face with
what he called a red-haired caveman. Boiler described dropping his
jaw and cocking his head to one side in disbelief. Surprisingly, the red-
haired caveman copied Boiler's exact head movement, and dropped its
jaw, and cocked its head to one side. However, Boiler explained it did
something with its eyes and body that made him think it wasn't
copying or mimicking him, it was mocking him. He went onto describe
this so unnerved him that he thought about grabbing the station-
issued sidearm he carried whilst off duty. He described how the thing
read his mind and knew what he was about to do before he made the
slightest of moves. It bolted off into the desert scrub brush. The story
gets even more exciting in what transpired after that moment, but it
doesn't help us understand the previous two trademark behaviors of a
common witness description, that being mimicry vs. emotional
intelligence, and hyper-alertness vs. omniscience. Both these qualities
were present in Boiler's retelling, and it left him wondering just what
in the hell was he dealing with. You can find the rest of the story on
SYFY's now-canceled series Paranormal Witness Season 1 | Watched
in the Woods.

I could tell Boiler was intrigued by the possibilities of what he met
that day, but he wanted immediate answers as to why he was never
told about them as a matter of cultural significance, at the very least.
After Boiler's incredible encounter he went back to the Sheriff's office
to tell his boss what he had just gone through. The Sheriff started to
laugh after he heard the first five seconds of Boiler's encounter. The
Sheriff explained that Deputy Boiler had seen what everyone else sees
on that side of the mountain without leaving a report.

2010

OZ

Unfortunately, the real estate crash of 2008 was too much for a struggling pizza restaurant way out in the woods to survive. The press coverage was not enough to keep the foreclosure walls crumbling around Ike's, and even with my efforts appreciated, soon Bigfoot & Beer would be no more.

On our last evening at the restaurant, I was closing out my tab and heading to my truck when a friend, Helen, came to me and said we have a couple of witnesses that don't want to be known and they need help. I walked over to the side of the parking lot by the dumpster and there I met Chad and Mary.

Mary introduced herself and her husband Chad as a local to the area and said, "We think we have Sasquatch in our backyard." I looked at Helen and then back to the witnesses. Mary described all their activity, as Chad mostly stood silently shaking his head. She described how they'd seen and heard something massive racing back and forth on the hillside and scaring the hell out of their pit bulls. They said, "Whatever it is, it has glowing eyes and runs like a shot." They asked us to come over as soon as possible and if we could, could we come by tonight. I asked Helen if she could join me and perhaps interview Mary while I interviewed her husband, Chad. When we got to their hidden home just off the highway, at least six roommates and three children all came running out, all talking at once about their own encounter story. We must have stood in the drive for an hour before we were taken to the back of the property that verged onto the forest edge.

That's where Helen escorted Mary, which left me trying to take in these witness testimonies by myself. The Children described seeing something watch them from the forest as they played on the trampoline. The roommates showed me 18-inch stick structures that looked like long leafless twigs bound in the middle with mud and pitch to look like crosses. They said they retrieved them in the forest behind their house. Chad said they found them one night when they scrambled up with their guns. I asked why they went up with guns and he said, "Because we have someone or something watching our kids and it's fucking pissing me off." I could tell Chad was not dealing with the phenomena like Mary was, and something told me we most likely won't be able to learn from their property for long.

It was soon after when night fell and Helen came walking back with Mary. Helen grabbed my shoulder and told me what she'd discovered from Mary and that we might want to spend time researching it later. It turns out Mary was a long-term witness of the phenomena and as a little girl on the Oregon Coast, had seen a Sasquatch watching her and her friend. It was masturbating. She was so grossed out by the childhood memory that she was alarmed her young daughters might have had the same horrific experience.

We told the family we would be back soon, and we would love to stay the evening and perhaps even go up the mountain to see what we could find. They agreed that would be fine and a mutual date was set. But the day passed by, as these things do. I would attempt to work out another day when all of us could scour their property and make our way up into the mountain, but unfortunately, the day never came. The hill behind their house was about four miles to the peak and would be a great spot for an overnight, but with Chad or Mary, it wasn't going to happen any time soon or ever.

I took matters into my own hands and discovered who owned most of the property on it. The 10s of thousands of acres of lumbar would for sure belong to a lumber company or BLM. Thankfully, I was wrong on both accounts. After asking around, I found out that four doors down from Mary and Chad lived a retired elderly guy named Earl. It was all his, and he was right there on the land. I drove down the road to a yellow double-wide nestled in the Doug Firs and knocked on the door. About nine feral cats came running off the patio as I shuffled back through empty popcorns and kitty shit. I could hear rummaging coming for the door. As the door opened an elderly man with a big neighborly smile asked, "How can I help ya?" I introduced myself to who I assumed was Earl and asked if the property behind his trailer leading to the hill was all his. He nodded and said, "What do you wanna know for?" I began to tell him my story and he told me his. It turns out Earl was a Naval badass with several tours in WWII and a huge photo album of all his deployments. He was in an early version of the Navy Seals before the actual USN Seals were formed. I could tell he had fond memories of spending most of his early 20s knee-deep in adventure. Honestly, I felt like a total wuss sitting there next to this military hero.

I was more than a little stuck about telling the rest of the story as to what I was there for. Finally, Earl did the job for me. He turned and looked at my Jeep and said, "Hey, I notice you have a Sasquatch bumper sticker on your rig. Hey Brandy," Earl belted, "go get the photos of the tracks we found." Brandy was Earl's fifty-year-old daughter who lived with them, her disabled son and bedridden mother. "Go get the photos of the tracks we found." I laughed and said, "No shit?" It wasn't more than a couple of minutes until Brandy came out with three color photos of bare-footed human-type tracks coming down from the hillside in the snow. The prints walked right out from the trees into the backfield and simply vanished. Earl's question to me was, "How did they do that?" I said, "I don't know, Earl, but if you give me permission to hike up there maybe we can all find out." Earl said, "not a problem," and permission was granted. He was ecstatic to have the company and wanted to share in a good ole crazy adventure perhaps one last time.

So within a couple of weeks, I was back and ready to hike up the infamous active mountain. I was offered a tour guide, that being Brandy's fifteen-year-old son who was on the spectrum somewhat. A very nice young man who knew how to hike and he was eager to get out from the watchful eye of his loving mother. So we packed up an overnight bag and headed up. After about two hours of uphill bushwhacking, we landed in a clearing, which seemed to be an old helipad landing with a now overgrown cleared-out area that was perfectly flat. We decided this would be the perfect spot to set up the tent before heading out to scout. We spread out the map and took a couple bites from a granola bar before walking up the old skid trail that led through some re-prod growth to an embankment that looked back over the valley we just hiked out of. It was the summer months, and the days were long. I broke out my binoculars to look down at the helipad we were set up at and I could not spot our tent. It could have been around a corner and tucked back out of my view, but I was sure I would see at least a piece of it. I told Brandy's son we had to go back to see if our tent was ok. He followed me back down; which wasn't far, only about fifteen minutes walking, and as we rounded the corner to the clearing we saw the tent was indeed gone. In fact, it had been moved over 50 feet and around a corner. It sat atop an 8-foot tall Rhododendron. It was even facing the same direction and right side up. I looked over at Brady's son whose mouth dropped open. I must say mine dropped lower than his. It was the middle of a cloudless summer day and there was no wind to blow that tent, let alone around a corner and 8 feet up. Not only that but the tent fly was also pulled off and moved forward away from where the tent had blown. The map was stashed on the ground loose and hadn't moved an inch. The candy wrapper from the granola bars hadn't moved. We were not alone, and someone had moved our tent in broad daylight. We played out every scenario, even the fact that a human had followed us up and moved our tent as a joke. We knew it wasn't Earl, even with all his years of experience as a SEAL, he was incapable in those days of climbing anywhere we went. Nobody knew of our plan except him and Brandy, and she was tasked as a full-time caregiver to her mom. But was it possible someone had just followed us to mess with us? In the coming months and years, I would conclude that this mountain held amazing secrets and dubbed it OZ. It had all the same characters inserted into a strange dreamlike world and it was capable of displaying magic. I was given complete freedom to study it as often as I wanted and I never wandered into anyone else up there who wasn't with me. This was for the better part of four years. Things I experienced in Oz:

1. Large phosphorous white lights exploding at close range. No sound experienced with them, or camera found at sight.
   They exploded four times moving in front of the trees from right to left at approx. 100 feet off the ground to as low as 15 feet.
2. Small pinpricks of white light bursting at approx. 5 feet off the ground.
3. Tree structures in the middle of old trails.
4. Small fresh dead rodents with blood still oozing out from

them. It appeared as though the animals were pinched in half and set on the trail.

5. Heavy stomping/running in my direction from behind during a hot summer day on an open trail. I turned around and saw that nobody was there.

6. Large human-like scat with bone and hair inside near one of Earl's lawnmowers. To the left and right of the scat were two human types of foot impressions on the lawn.

OZ

Brandy would describe seeing large shadows outside her window while she was watching tv. In the morning, she went outside to investigate and would find objects laid outside her window. They usually looked like small irrelevant items or scraps you would find in the junkyard or abandoned campsite.

Mary and Chad heard about the lights we saw up above the property and called to say she'd also seen lights, even on the same night as we had. Mary described small solid balls of white light that would come through their bedroom window at night.

Earl, the last I checked, is still doing fine but is now a widower. Brandy's son went to jail for drug possession and resisting arrest. The property went through a couple of land sales to local timber companies and an eventual wildfire that almost burned the entire hillside to ash.

Shortly after my adventure at Oz, I reached back out to Roger's. I explained what I witnessed and he laughed before saying, "I told you so, be careful." Besides him, I knew nobody else local I could regularly count on to bounce things off. I was for the most part solo looking into this all. My son was too young and leery of the woods. He was also struggling medically with an auto-immune disorder holding him back from anything physical.

FEB. 2012
THE LONDON FOG

The cold wind and rain poured down in frigid temps over the lake basin. Moss and driftwood covered the emptied muddy lake bottom along with fifteen other people taking shifts in documenting and plaster casting the large deep footprints that had been found. These were the London Tracks, and they were initially discovered by a fella named Max Roy. Without going into the convoluted details, Max Roy made note of these tracks and showed them to my son and his mother. I was then contacted right after Max visited my son and told about the tracks. I then went down to the lake with a friend and immediately considered the footprints to be worthy of casting as a possible Sasquatch trackway. What was initially thought of as three or four prints on the lake ridge would soon be outnumbered by over a hundred and eighteen other matching footprints that walked off the ridge and out into the drained lake. Over a five-day period on a rain-soaked week, fifteen people helped document a single trackway that spread over 100 yards off the lakebed and into a semi-circle. Eight years have gone by and to this day we don't know definitively who made them. The London Trackway is unique in behavior for known Sasquatch tracks. The cast themselves look very unusual and don't match other known casts that have been shown. Incredible circumstances exist about the trackway characteristics that cannot be duplicated easily, or at all, by a hoaxer. The 40-inch step in the mud for over 80 yards without another impression in the wet slippery mud. The lack of a significant heel impression for someone running in a rigid or pliable cut-out stomper. The efforts by others who've used stompers to hoax tracks with a great distance between them have had to utilize the help of aerial devices, an accomplice, or heavy machinery. In the end and rather quickly the jig is up, and their names are known. Soon after these tracks were cast and disseminated out to those who helped themselves, another trackway of similar size was found near Elbe, Washington. The tracks were discovered to be a hoax and a throw down to the London Tracks. It was curious that the hoaxer was discovered so quickly through hunting down emails and IP addresses, but the London Tracks remained a solid mystery.

There were unsubstantiated rumors of a nearby lonely landscaper who'd been blamed for taking credit. The rumor was he did it all with diving flippers. He fooled a lot of folks with a very crude excuse. I have my doubts as to the tracks being hoaxed, but that's because of what I now know of the land and its true nature.

LONDON TRACKWAY

1. As of 2012, it was the largest single trackway cast in a lakebed. Over 122 plaster prints cast partly or complete.
2. It was cast over five days in a complete weather deluge, largely at night.
3. It was cast on private property owned and managed by the ACoE - Army Corps of Engineers.
4. There were no other visible tracks or impressions on the lakebed other than 14.5-inch barefooted human-type tracks.

5. The tracks were over 40 and sometimes over 50 inches in width from toe to heel.

6. There was a noted lack of a deep heel impression and a very present gripping of the toes.

7. Most tracks were cast in the lakebed, which quickly filled with rainwater atop mossy topsoil.

8. The tracks were almost perfectly inline or "tight rope" steps with only occasional slide-outs, and one 90 degrees angle left turn on the ball of the right foot.

9. The lakebed tracks were never reported to anyone. The initial three steps on the ridge were all witness Max Roy mentioned.

10. There is a reported lack of toe spreading and closing between each step.

11. No known significant dermal or skin wrinkles.

12. No known hair sample was gathered and tested.

13. The reported tracks photographed were close to a local fishing hole.

14. People who helped document the London Tracks reported seeing others across London Road coming from private property, which included 5-foot tall barb wire fences. These claims were never documented.

15. Tracks cast were left in the rain during the evening while we cleaned up at a neighboring motel. During that night the tracks were stolen.

16. The Army Corps of Engineers never went on the record to help us or deter our efforts.

17. The personal contact of Cliff Barackman from Hood River, Oregon, who performed a weight displacement study on the track maker's total weight in lbs. never made his results public. He told me privately over the phone after tracking him down, that the tracks made no sense as far as weight. He went on to say the tracks were 500+ lbs. in weight and that his calculations must have been off. This news was never documented or publicized as far as I know.

18. Cliff Barackman has since given his entire casted prints from London Trackway to Sasquatch Author Thom Powell.

For more info on the London Tracks read Thom Powell's book Edges of Science. He was on the ground with us and wrote extensively about the circumstances surrounding the find. Thom is known for writing more fringe than most with the evidence surrounding Sasquatch interaction. As it would turn out, The London Tracks would lead to an event that would give Thom quite a bit of "fringe" material.

Five days after the London find, and the tracks were cast, taken, and dispersed, our new group met at the local pub to discuss the details of the possibilities. I remember one Sunday evening around 11 pm, we left that pub and headed up a ridge-line above the lakebed. Two locals to Cottage Grove named John and Todd, who also helped cast and track some of the lakeside impressions, were to be the leaders in this night venture. They suggested heading up a gated road on foot and then hiking to the top where their sighting and experiences had happened years back. We walked in as a group to the gate and immediately separated as we climbed up a long and steep graveled logging road.

As we headed up the road, I barked back down the hill that we should kill our headlamps and use what was left of the moon as our guide. A moon that was at that hour blanketed by a rainstorm.

As I approached the middle where a Y separated the road into three legs, I waited for the crew to catch up. I was eager for adrenaline, and it seemed that I was carting around old farts who couldn't handle the sudden cardio workout. Then, one by one, they made it up the road and awaited the next grouping. There were six in total, including myself. After about ten minutes or so we stood under the Doug Firs in the dark. Five of us waited for the sixth. Fifteen minutes, twenty minutes go by. Then at around thirty minutes, my phone rings a text. It was John. His text read something like, "I didn't feel it was a good idea to go up that road tonight. I am home now...not sure why?" We didn't know what to make of that and wondered if it was something medical or emotional, but not once did we consider more suspicious reasons for his sudden departure.

We split into two groups. One group of three and the other group with two. The group of three comprised Helen, who I wrote about in the Oz location, Todd, a local Grover, which by the way is a respectable term for locals born and raised in Cottage Grove, and then lastly, a new guy named Dylan.

In the two-man group, there was me and Dave. Dylan and Dave, as I mentioned, were a last-minute decision, but they had shown up some years back at Bigfoot & Beer and I'd promised them that if I ever came close to seeing a Sasquatch, I would try and get them to come along.

I decided they would be a great fit and I knew they could handle themselves in the woods. They both worked for the state as first responders and were trained pros in stressful situations. Although neither had ever seen a Sasquatch, or had any known experience with the paranormal, they wanted to, and would drive two hours at a moment's notice, to hike in the cold night for a shot in the dark. That was good enough for me and the gang.

Helen, Todd, and Dylan headed down the hill as Dave and I hiked up. If anything super strange would happen then at least Dylan and Dave would have an advocate with them to explain the possibilities. Helen was privy to her strange sightings well before I met her. She was confident almost in an irresponsible way that would sometimes get her in binds, but never enough to keep her away from her signature confidence and assuredness. Todd was a two-time Sasquatch witness who took no rumor for granted surrounding the strange stories of Cottage Grove. Todd was also, in my estimation, a Shaman trapped in a Redneck. There was something about Todd's approach that I admired. He, like Helen, had a swagger about him in the woods, however, there is more here, much more. He was also a bit reckless and dangerous. A quality that comes in handy when trying to study the phenomena at close range.

Dave and I headed up past the surging crackle of the field power lines. We sought shelter from an ever-present rainstorm chasing after us with every step. Soon we found ourselves hiding under the extended umbrella of old-growth forest. A perfect place we could both sit and possibly wait out the relentless rain. I don't mind the good fortune of precipitation, but this was punishing. It was nearly 11:30 pm by the time Dave and I reached the trees and we both sat down on a semi-dry piece of deadwood. Dave and I talked about a recent friend who'd died unexpectedly and how strange it was to have them go in such a tragic manner. We listened to the possible sounds of sticks break down the hill. Each moment pausing in our conversation to note the sounds and train our ears.

Then suddenly, without notice, Dave bends down off the log and onto his knees. He then crouches down in the wet gravel and lays flat on his stomach. As he lays there he continues to slowly talk and listen. I am watching him now more than the woods. His body was flat and supine to the ground, in the water and mud. I watch him closely, noting the fact he was wearing recon gear that's generally pricey. The kind of gear that looks more like indoor fashion than outdoor fatigue.

His hands brace the forest floor like he is getting ready to crawl someplace, but why and where?

We stop talking as I watch him and the tree-line. Then he says, "Did ya hear that?"

I said, "Maybe, not sure…where?" Dave whispered, "That way" and points up the way into the pitch-black night. I suggested we may want to approach on foot. His eyes narrow and transfixed on a section of woods. "Dave, hey let's get up and walk over there," I insisted. He mumbles something and gets up with me, his body now dripping with cold mud. As we walk up the road maybe 9 feet, Dave slowly and apprehensively approached from behind and to my right. He was moving so carefully that it made me rethink his participating.

I was nervous for him, and the air was thick with suspicion. Dave moved as though we were walking through an IED field, or a sniper was tracking us. He looked the part too, like a war-torn Army Ranger sneaking over enemy lines. Then all at once, he said something out of character, "I can't take another step." I was immediately flooded with witness accounts I'd heard over the years of what they call The Dread Response. This is the theory that whatever is going on re: the phenomena of the paranormal or Sasquatch, it can immobilize and target individuals. I use the word target because just like a bullet, it's said to be aimed. I felt nothing as I watched Dave wither under assumed non-friendly fire. Dave stood silently with his eyes glaring into the black hallway of trees ahead. "I can't take another step, I feel like throwing up."

Yet another classic symptom of The Dread Response is abdominal pain and immobility. I take a deep breath and look over with my headlamp now on. I decide it's time to explain what I've heard re: his symptoms. "Dave, you may be getting zapped!"

Dave lowered his head but looked dead ahead from under his brow-line. His breath became quicker now and his hands wrapped around his pack straps.

"I'm gunna cry, why the fuck am I gunna cry?" Dave moaned.

I begin to assume this isn't going to be an easy midnight stroll and I better buckle up.

"Dave," I say, "if something is trying to push you out of here, then let's try and push back. Take a couple more steps with me." Dave stammered his words as he agreed and reluctantly says, "O.K." With that, we took one step and he stopped again. "I can't, why the hell am I gunna cry? This is fucking bullshit!" To be transparent, I was pissed and worried that I'd brought out a real nutcase that might have been having a mental breakdown. Perhaps a triggered PTSD episode from his work was brought out via a moment in the dark.

In the moments between fighting back tears and nearly vomiting for no apparent reason, Dave then says this, "THEY, want me to leave!" I turned my head back to him and replied, "huh, what did you just say?" Dave again stammered, "I can't take another step, they want me to leave!"

If this wasn't being zapped or the Dread Response, then this was either a full mental collapse or an unknown chemical reaction. Whichever way, it was all getting worse and although I wanted to move forward, it was obvious I had to assess my friend and 180 out of there.

Dave walked behind me and slumped his head down tucked into his shoulders like a turtle. He outpaces me as he briskly walked down the hill. The trees still surrounding us, Dave murmurs, "What the hell is this, what's happening. THEY asked me to leave?" I listen and follow. I grab my radio and call the other group who we found waiting at the Y-axis. Dave's shoulders are up above his ears and his voice is quaking as he looks for only one thing on the road, a way back! He grabs his partner, Dylan, by the shirt collar and said, "I'm leaving, WE'RE leaving, together!" And with that, they both looked back down the hill as I hear the two exchanging expletives. We yell down the hill as they slipped around the corner, "Call us later and we will check on ya."

I explained to Helen and Todd what had happened, knowing both could be witnesses and experiencers of the Dread Response or being zapped, they would get why tonight was shaping up the way it looked.

The three of us stood out in the frigid night on the side of the gravel bar. I related the details of my experience with Dave. They both repeated almost in unison, "THEY zapped him!"

I leaned in, agreeing with both, and wondered how we would fair going back up, into what most folks would call the "no go zone."

Just to be clear, all three of us are adrenaline junkies. Drugs never were my thing and as far as I knew then, Helen and Todd had only the occasional beer or joint. Helen looked at me, calling me her little brother, "So little brother, ya ready to go back up?" Todd was already on his way as she chided. I buckled my pack and gripped my walking stick, "Yes, are ya kidding?"

However, this was ominous and just left a full-grown man in tears. Yet, we saw nothing and had little experience with being zapped. As we crossed out from under the power lines and into the tree line where the rain shed down onto the branches of The Doug Firs, I stopped them and said, "This is the spot, this was where it all went down." We all walked past this supposed demarcation line and waited to get hit. Then, with a single step, all focus changed, and the road became alien. I will try to describe this as close to the feeling as possible, but I may fall short due to there being no human words for this moment.

In a single step, I dipped into what felt like a vertical wall of unseen submission. It was like walking into a wall of Jello, or what I imagine a moonwalk would feel like. The air became thick and weighed with gravity. My body walked fully into the alien air, and I could only slowly react with a delayed movement. I looked up and behind and saw Todd. He was watching his hands as they entered with his body.

His steps were slow and deliberate. We both comment on what we're feeling as we continue walking up the road. It reminded me of trying to walk on the bottom of a deep swimming pool.

I turn my head to the left and see Helen walking beside us unaffected. I hear her comment regarding her "extra senses" her Spidey tingle is telling her, "they are watching us!"

She starts moving quickly up the mountain and watching us as we slowly push through the thick air. I recall saying something, and I'm not sure what to make of it, but I said it nonetheless. "They're going to let us come up." I turn back to see Todd still behind and both push through the invisible force. If this was the dread response Dave was answering, then we were feeling it a whole lot differently.

Helen scrambles past us, almost ignoring our circumstances, and disappears into the trees. She's talking to someone but not us. We sludge through the air and just to the top of an old log landing. As we enter the clearing I feel my arm swing fast, then my legs and body. I was exiting the force, just like you would if you climbed out of a swimming pool. There was no sound and nothing visual, just a feeling. I am free. I turn around to see Todd right behind me push past the same invisible wall. First his head, arms, legs, and body.

Todd walks to me in the rainy night air, his arms extended, and palms faced up. He looks into the surrounding woods and turns in circles, "THEY don't like that I brought my pistol." I watch him as I see Helen tramp deeper into the woods. She calls out to us, "Guys, they're right here if ya want to see them."

At this point, I feel as though I'm in a dream that should soon end with the alarm beep. What in the fuck did I just experience and for Christ's sake, can I get a breather from the weirdness before the next crazy-ass assertion. But I was guilty, I said THEY will let us come up. THEY? They, what, who, come on!

Todd is now in full hypnotic trance mode. His eyes bugged out and were still turning in circles with his palms facing up. Not anything you would ever see in a typical redneck Grover. "Todd! Hey," Helen whispers, "there's a Sasquatch over there behind that tree line." He stops turning and walks her way, I slowly follow scanning the trees and sky.

I hear Helen still speaking to an unseen body. We walk past the low-hanging tree branches soaked with rain that only serves as a wet face slap as we seek dry shelter. We were soaked from head to toe, every layer drenched.

Helen is kneeled on the edge of a fern growth looking down into the re-prod of skinny trees. The darkness providing cover to what she can barely see, and we cannot. Her words are very friendly and speak to them like neighbors over for beers, "Hey y'all, these two guys only want to know what I already know, that you're God's creation and that you can teach them your beautiful ways." I see nothing and only watch where she watches, Todd the same. We both sit to the side of her and wait to see something. She points, "They're right there guys, I just saw the eyes glow." Still, I see nothing.

Then, something smooth and warm slides over my head. Like a sedative being slipped or sleeping gas filling the air. All at once, I went from a massive adrenaline dump to now being lulled to sleep. I ask if anyone else feels something happening, I hear Todd reply yes. We both comment on feeling drowsy and wanting to lay down on the wet sloped hill.

I sit legs crossed in a puddle and begin to lay down, Todd the same. Todd comments, "THEY are mad I brought my pistol; they want me to get rid of my pistol." I hear the words but don't respond. Todd unbuttons his holster and looks like he grabs the handle. Then Helen barks out, "Don't you dare throw that gun, that gun is his for his safety so he can protect his family, himself, and us." Todd hears her and quickly snaps his holster button. It was like a trance unbroken by common sense. We're both still tired and feel the rush of sleep pushing down from our heads to our toes like a plunger in a syringe.

Helen sees what's happening to us and yells again to the woods "knock it off." Right after she yells, we begin to rouse. I feel the rise of blood pumping and adrenaline surging. Then Todd says something way out of place for a good ole boy. "I'm gunna be sick because I brought my gun, I shouldn't have brought my gun." His breathing returns from the spell and he's animated but seemingly nauseous. "I have to go, I can't do this shit no more, I can make it down on my own," Todd forcefully says. "Like hell," I said; "nobody's going back alone!" Helen stands up and I stand beside her, Todd still sitting. We help him up and take an arm over each shoulder. Helen conversationally commenting as we leave the trees. As we walk down with Todd still in our arms, he takes command of his composure and limps beside us as we all briskly walk down and past the point where it all started. Periodically, as we walked, we felt something like a mutual scan over us. We all comment on it as we head down, hearing nothing.

As we get to the truck and we all hop in and lock the door, Helen grabs a beer and Todd and I light a smoke. Nobody said anything much, we all just breathed heavy and fogged up the truck windows. If we did speak at all it was unremarkable and our main concern was getting Todd out of there. He grabs the steering wheel and revs the engine. "I'm going home." He drives off as Helen and I stand outside my vehicle, wondering if we should go back up. After all, for the most part, I was fascinated more than frightened. For Helen, it was just another day. She said as we left, "Well that was sure interesting, little brother."

We head back to my house and stayed up until morning reliving the past week and the long, unusual night. As Helen airs out her wet clothes for the dryer, she notices a glove missing. She says, "Damn, I liked those gloves." Losing articles of outwear is fairly common on night walks or night sits.

The next day we call author Thom Powell and author Joe Beelart, both authors of Sasquatch books. Thom Powell is like the best of wit and intellect, bottled up in a tall and spry sixty-year-old science teacher. Joe Beelart I knew less of, but my impression of him was he liked Thom enough to come down and see the Sasquatch evidence no matter how strange it sounded.

Once both guys arrived in town, Helen met them and showed them the trackway and the area where the weirdness took place. I had to work, but they explored the scene and found Helen's missing glove. It was sitting in the gravel road with two sticks on top in an X.

After about three or four days of silence, I heard from Todd and Dave. They described an intense feeling of being sick and tired, like they underwent a trauma of sorts, or PTSD. They came out from under it all eventually, but I believe that for those two, especially in the eyes of their friends and family, their normal world had been wrecked.

As for me, well it shaped my suspicions that there's more to the supernatural than expected. Yes, I felt strange forces occur that evening, but it wasn't foreboding. I did wonder whether or not it was a mass hysteria-based soul on adrenaline. Was I so suggestible that I could have had physical reactions to a mass delusion? Basically, seeing and feeling what I was being told to see and feel? I wasn't high or drunk, but maybe others were around me and that explains their paranoia. To be honest, I'm still confused about that night and can't say with certainty what happened. Never sure of how or why, but utterly assured of the details.

Summer 2013
Blue Suede Shoes

After that event in the mountains, there was no turning back as to what was possible. By now, with everything that had happened in the last six years, I was still reminded of Rodger's initial comment "the rest of the story is far too weird." It replayed in my head every day as I thought about what I was starting to believe. It was changing me, and it was showing.

Eventually, the story of the London Tracks reached national media and a production company wanted the exclusive. I consulted Todd about this and wanted to get his opinion on it all. Why would I consult Todd? Well, since our group moment on the ridge above the lake it became clear Todd felt out of control. The woods of Cottage Grove were his home, and that home was now scary and being eyed by a major cable network. I knew all this was somehow aimed at me as the ringleader of Sasquatch tourism and he didn't like it. He let me know. So I spoke with him and even if Todd protested, they would still come and film anywhere the state forest permitted them. However, this commercialism of the London Tracks and Sasquatch led Todd and me down an important road. One that was to help me understand the complexity and thoughtfulness of an unknown being.

After filming was finished, Todd was tipped off by one of the show's hosts about a nearby location he may want to follow up on. The area was about an hour past Ike's Pizza in the Cascade Mountain Range. It was in this location the film crew was shooting b-roll footage and looking into possible local sighting reports. A single cameraman and the host stay a couple of nights in this spot to see what transpires. As they bed down in their respective tents, they both place their boots outside under the fly. The host, as tradition, sets out a gifted necklace on the toe of his boot. The cameraman leaves nothing gifted only his boots. The next morning the cameraman finds a beaded leather necklace on the toe of his boot and wakes the host to see if he had left it there. The host unzips his tent to see his necklace is untaken and the cameraman is holding a different necklace. The cameraman passes it off as simple crow or raven behavior, but the host does not. He relates his belief to Todd that it was Sasquatch who pulled this off. Todd, who was usually between jobs like me, grabbed his son who was out of school for the summer and takes off to this location for the week.

They brought along a tent, fishing gear, and backpacks. They were to stay for days and see just how close a Sasquatch would get, if at all. They waited a couple of days and then moved to another nearby sight where a natural spring poured freely out the hillside. The area was off-grid camping for sure and surrounded by huge old-growth Doug Firs and a nearby rushing creek. It was only about an hour's drive into the Oregon Three Sisters Wilderness where tens of thousands of acres of forest, lava flow, and underground caves are nature's playground.

As Todd and his son build a fire, they start hearing calls off in the distance. The night was falling, and it would be a good time to flashlight up and head out to the sounds on foot. So they packed up from the campsite, built a nice sized fire to keep stoked while away, and walked into the night. As they got to a dried-up creek bed they heard rocks suddenly crashing nearby. They quickly learned the rocks were being tossed, if not aimed, near them. They exploded on impact and the message was very clear, LEAVE! They did in haste and walked the nearby logging road back to camp. As they walked in the night, they heard parallel in the woods the sound of bi-pedal walking. The dense brush failed to slow the cadence of each large footstep. They would both stop and shine their lights into the trees, expecting to catch a predator or perhaps even the impossible. The footsteps would stop as they stopped, almost to the degree of predicting when they would both hit the brakes.

They walked briskly back to the glow of the fire and waited through the night. As they did, Todd's son learned of the immediacy of their new night visitors. Son and Father sitting beside a fire awaiting more signs, soon a small pinecone would land near the son and roll near his feet. The boy talked to his father about what just occurred and Todd noted shadows dashing behind huge nearby down trees as sounds and objects came closer to the firelight.

Todd tells his son, "Let's change gears boy." The son now wide-eyed, turns to Dad and says, "just how do ya expect I can do that? I just had a small rock hit my shoe." Todd says, "Ok, I'll start first... basketball season starts soon, ya?" His son looks dismayed at the redirection and says, "ya, so?" Todd burst out, "Well, ya need anything for the season? Money is tight this year so I need to know now so I can save up." His son replies, "If I have to talk about this now then I guess I need shoes. The shoes I have now are all I have." Todd noted and said, "Roger that...shoooooes!" Todd's son had all he could take of the diversion and exclaimed, "Dad, I'm done getting shit thrown at me, and to be honest I'm getting mad and pissed off." Todd's son may have been all of fourteen at the time but he was his father's kid through and through, just like his Dad, being taught to take no shit and go on the offense early.

Todd had no time to react as his son grabbed a small rock from the ground and tossed it at their shadowy assailants who lay beyond two-hundred-year-old deadfall. Poor choice perhaps, because then all hell broke loose. Immediately, the boy felt threatened and sickly as the fire was returned and the feeling of dread swept into the thoughts of a young man now unmatched. Todd knew this feeling well from only nine months back after the London Tracks. He told his son, "We're leaving and we're leaving now!" He left every possession they'd packed and gunned the Dodge for the safety of the highway. That's when I got the call.

As Todd was retelling the entire night's events, I heard in the background his son repeating the same words. Then, he said something very odd. "Dad, why do I taste cherry tomatoes?" I asked, "Todd, what did he just say?" Todd asked, "What did ya say son about tomatoes?"

His son said again, "I taste cherry tomatoes in my mouth, did you dip my cigar in a tomato paste?" Todd replied, "what are you talking about son?" I then yelled over both of them as I heard the engine growl, "Dude, is your kid smoking a cigar?" Todd replied, "Oh ya, but it's just a Backwoods...he's saying he tastes tomatoes in his mouth." This conversation, although confusing and pointless, would soon come into play.

Todd and his son went home, and the plan was for me to see them around 9 am the next day. We packed into his Dodge and headed back to the abandoned camp. I knew immediately that Todd leaving all his fishing and camping gear behind meant there was a legit emergency to get out and run. As we pulled up to the single road, we noted a mud flat still flooded, so we got out and looked for tracks. We saw two barefoot prints immediately, small and in line headed off the road into the natural spring nearly at the hill.

We noted it and flagged the area. Then they showed me the scene and the rocks and cones that came in, as well as the area where they were followed back and then something curious happened. About 150 yards deep in the dense forest was a small plastic back hanging about 5 feet up in the trees. The bag was filled with Cherry tomatoes. We looked at the site where the bag had been pinched open from the bottom and you could see fingerprints where the plastic was ripped apart. Below the bag is a 5x5 area of smashed ferns and moss. On the moss and ferns was the skin of the tomatoes that had been eaten. They were scattered around directly under the bag. Nothing was left in the bag, they'd all simply been sucked of juice and the skins left. We collected what we could from the area and cast the two smaller prints. As we were casting the tracks I asked Todd, "Did your boy put any tomatoes in his pocket for hiking?" He said, "Son did ya pack any tomatoes off for our hike?"

The boy said, "No, but I sure did taste em last night, weird eh." I said, "Ya, really weird."

Todd said, "Hey son, why don't ya take this plastic bag and hang up some dog food where the tomatoes were, maybe ya can make peace with them." Son answered, "Ya mean, make peace with what... Sasquatch? Ya think they give a shit about that?" Todd replied, "I've got no clue, but it wouldn't hurt to try." Todd's son begrudgingly leaves the casting of the tracks and walks off into the woods alone. We keep an eye on him as far as we can see around the ancient fallen logs.

The tracks dried nice enough to where we could pull them and leave. As we pulled the prints, we heard a stammering voice come walking back from the tree line. Todd's son had a pair of sneakers in his hands. "Dad, look what I found by the cherry tomato spot, they weren't there forty minutes ago." Todd to son, "Where did ya find those?" His son answered, "They were right where we just saw all the skins of the tomato." I said, "Wait...what? Where?" Todd's son walked us both to the exact spot where he found them. He sets the shoes near the log he found them at. It was the exact spot we were just on our hands and knees. We examined the area and looked for anything that could have snuck up on us and left them. Nothing was obvious about this. We grabbed the shoes and examined them. They were about size 10 blue suede Converse low-top sneakers. They had moss layered over the outside and a bit inside. They smelled musky like they were kept in an enclosed area for a long period. Todd and I looked at one another.

BLUE SHOES

"There's no way we could have missed those," I said. "No way," Todd's son agreed.

Then it hit all three of us at once. The conversation, the redirection conversation around the campfire last night. Shoes, the son needed shoes, and now here are shoes. The necklace was left on the boot for the cameraman. Could it be linked? Any of it? Hell, it was even the kid's size?

We collected the camping gear, the tracks, and the shoes. Funny enough, Todd suggested his son wear the shoes for basketball season to see if it helped his 3-pointers, but the son never did. In fact, he never did wear those shoes and they may well have got lost in the shuffle of growing out of them. Perhaps growing out of the beauty of that encounter and all that it represented.

2013-2016
PUMP THE BREAKS

During this time, life was complicated, and I stepped away from any deep research. I got married and divorced again. I went through a huge three-year legal battle, moved three times, all while my son was battling an autoimmune illness that eventually pulled him out of public school. All this and I was working fifty hours a week. There was no time for Sasquatch, and it was almost taboo to bring it up. Nobody in my family cared about anything you just read and to be honest I didn't want to talk about it either. I shelved it all and privately stewed on where my life was and where it was headed. I knew it wasn't all over but couldn't shape how to re-engage with the same approach. I had to get my independence and autonomy back from the world so I could be a free agent. I felt slowed down by routine norms and became deeply depressed. It showed and I was a bad fit for typical suburban life. So, I exited the world's expectations placed upon me and sold everything to start fresh.

I bought a small 16-foot camper and a Jeep and moved out to the country. My son was only about fifteen minutes away and we'd spend my days going out for breakfast when he was feeling well. Usually, he would have been my go hiking buddy during my days off, but now his health just wasn't capable of the efforts. Also, and not mentioned in previous pages, was his brief encounter and sighting near an area called the French Pete wilderness. It was only about an hour away from the blue suede shoe spot where he and I were with a couple of friends mushroom picking. I knew the area was rich with Sasquatch history, but I never thought one would come right up to our camp and watch the kids. Well, that, in a nutshell, is what my son described. They were scared by the sighting, and it leveled any chance of getting him to embrace this world again, even when he was feeling well. I tried a couple more times to re-introduce him to the mystery, but it filled his mind with anxiety and stress, which is the last thing you want with an autoimmune issue.

I drove semi-truck up and down the interstate and listened to a lot of podcasts re: the supernatural and paranormal. If these podcasts were books, I would have read thousands of pages as I drove thousands of miles. Eventually, I would have to re-immerse myself back into the world, it called to me as I drove past pristine forests and mountains. There are always conferences or campouts one can visit to fill the void of not going full-time in the woods.

It was during a 2017 conference I met someone who would shape my understanding of how different life could be. Someone who told me a different story of myself and the reality of magic. It was with her that life took on a deeper meaning and we both slowly fell in love.

Speaking not in the past tense of our relationship today, I will describe her in those terms for the sake of our meeting. She owns a room when she walks into it. There are other directions to gaze at towards Eryn's fierce beauty and wit. She was a model, equestrian, self-made businesswoman, and a Sasquatch expedition leader for the BFRO...as well as an extended experiencer. When I met her, I knew none of this, but I could tell she was brilliant, so I simply approached her and reached out my hand. It was that handshake that changed my heart from attracted to compelled. In the coming weeks and months, we would become great friends and date from afar. Her living in Washington and me still in Oregon. It sure couldn't last this way and eventually one of us had to move.

Meanwhile, as life rebuilt around me I was reminded of an anniversary soon approaching. The 2017 anniversary of The London Tracks was now five years old. I put out an online post about this and again engaged the locals of Cottage Grove to meet me down at the lake if they had clues as to if the tracks were hoaxed by a nearby prankster. To this day, nobody has ever taken me up on that offer. However, one person did contact me online. His name was Darrell Adam and he'd just purchased a house down past the lakebed. He seemed to know a lot about the area and all things Sasquatch-related.

As he described where he lived, he mentioned he was lucky enough to buy a two-story farmhouse for an incredible price. He also recently retired and had an open schedule, and would love to meet up at the lakebed. So, in February 2018, we meet up at the empty lakebed and swap Sasquatch stories. I was still not a first-hand witness but Darrell and his brother were. He wanted to know more about the subject, and I think he looked at it as a natural fit for the recently retired. We set a time and place to go back up behind his home, a road I knew had previously reported sightings. One involved four eyewitnesses that watched three Sasquatch leave the tree line as another bigger one provided cover. Hell, all the locals knew they were up that way too and it was known as a hotspot for night drives in search of Sasquatch. I told Darrell all of this and he said, "Well, show me, man." I laughed and said, "No problem man, but you gotta know something. Once you hang out with me, you have to know what we're looking for is largely supernatural. This will affect what people think of you, once they find that out, and especially once they discover you're hanging with me." He assured me he didn't care and can make up his mind regarding the mystery and who he hangs out with.

Also, during this time of transition near the town of Dorena, I met a family of extended experiencers, Lisa and Shaun Phay. They had incredible stories of interaction on their property. The hill behind their house was all national forest and the river in front was known by local gold miners as a frequent spot for brief encounters. It was between the Phay's and Adam's property that I would find my new approach. I had to organize yet another spot for us all to meet and network, something like Bigfoot & Beer but with more diverse unusual content.

Around January 2018, I started Strange Bräu Radio in a small little historic bar called The Axe & Fiddle in downtown Cottage Grove, Oregon. It would be our monthly meet-up spot with guest speakers presenting on everything from local ghost stories and alien abduction to cryptos. The name itself was a tip of the hat to my German heritage, Bräu being the German ale or bar house.

2

MEETING THE ADAMS

Darrell invited me over to his home to meet him and his wife Cindy. They had an adorable miniature Aussie Sheppard name Izzy who greeted me with unmatched energy. I came inside and had a cup of coffee while I learned more about the Adamses. It turned out they'd gotten the house from a family who'd lived there for over fifteen years and raised all their teenage kids. They suddenly put the house on the market, sold it for a lot less than the asking price, and moved only 45 minutes down the road. Within only a month or two after moving, the family's oldest son put a gun to his head. The Adams had no idea why they moved so quickly or why there was a sudden suicide. They showed me photos of the family but it was only a giant family, in every shot smiling and hugging in the very kitchen we were all standing in. I thought it was odd and tragic, worth noting and perhaps following up on later.

They walked me around the house and the empty bedrooms with storage boxes. There was nothing on the walls, no framed photos or usual tchotchke's. It was just the two of them, the dog, and a giant tv in front of a couch with a single recliner. I wondered to myself, had they planned on flipping the house for a profit and therefore hadn't unpacked fully.

Darrell took me outside and showed me the front of this home, which mainly faced a paved logging road, tall Fir trees, and their large gravel driveway. To the right and left of the house were a separated car garage and an unfinished metal shop. The backyard had a small grass lawn for the dog to run on with only a couple of trees and a small garden. It was separated by a 4-foot wire deer fence that neighbored an abandoned apple orchard. This was the same orchard that housed a Yurt home to a single mom. About five hundred yards up another long gravel drive was her father who lived by an old spring-fed creek. The only place immediately close to the Adams was an old farmhouse right next to them. A cedar fence was all that kept them apart. The house belonged to the father by the creek and it just sat unoccupied until it was rented shortly after the Adamses moved in.

It was a beautiful spot and had privacy, but it was far from town, and one would have to make sure they checked their grocery list before coming home. Also, when you live like this your cell phone and internet connection are up to the Gods. Sometimes the Adamses could get a good signal and sometimes not. Before I left, Darrell suggested I come back soon. He'd drawn an elk tag for an early hunt on a section of land above his home. He also mentioned that if the hunt went south we could go check out some possible Sasquatch tree structures he found. He showed me photos he'd taken of giant X formations composed of small Oak limbs. Most of the time, snow load explains suspect tree structures, but the area is steeped in sighting reports. I decided to take him up on his offer and explore a possible section of forest very near to the infamous wall of Jello mentioned before.

3

UNDER THE OWL MOON

W e met around 8 am on Good Friday of March 30th, 2018. The weather was perfect for a morning hunt with almost zero cloud cover and medium temperature. It was also a full moon that night, or what was known as The Owl Moon. We headed up in Darrell's pickup as we both ran binoculars over the landscape looking for signs worth scoping. We explored several areas I'd never been, but also other areas I had, especially areas where reliable Sasquatch sightings had been reported. As far as the hunting went, there was nothing legal to shoot. Around noon we sat on his tailgate and had lunch. We traded weird stories like boys with baseball cards. Darrell told me that he and Cindy lived in an incredibly haunted home and had everything from apportations, knocks and even ectoplasm fall through the ceiling and land right in front of Cindy in the kitchen. I asked Darrell what Cindy did when she saw this ethereal goo drip down to a blob in front of her feet? He goes on to tell me that, "Cindy doesn't care about that. She grabbed a dustpan and swept it into the trash can." I was a little flabbergasted at that hasty move. It made no sense in my way of thinking. It's such a rare thing to witness and how could you not collect it for the equivalent of show and tell? Cindy just isn't that type of person and Darrell knew if he found anything out of the ordinary it would more than likely just fall off her shrugged shoulder.

Around 2 pm we decided it was best to give up on the deer and move into stick structure mode. Darrell knew of a road I'd never taken and claimed to see large, crossed trees and logs that made distinct shapes. I was game, even if it was fruitless I knew this spot was close to a 2011 sighting where three Sasquatch were witnessed by four people on a full moon night. As a matter of synchronicity, tonight was also a full moon. A moon called The Owl Moon. It was also Good Friday before Easter. The weather was perfect, with blue skies and around 75 degrees. I sat shotgun in Darrell's truck and hung my head out the window looking for an elk or possible Sasquatch sign.

As we narrowed a corner winding up a clay embankment, I saw something out of the corner of my eye. I did a double-take and told Darrell to back up for a second. He hit the brakes and backed up to see what's going on. I leaned back and cocked my head as we backed to the point of interest. Right below my rolled-down window was a red clay bank with two divots on the ground. They were much larger than a typical sign of wildlife and looked peculiar. I asked Darrell to get out of the truck and look with me. We stopped the truck and we both crossed over to the 2 divots. They were only about two feet away from the gravel road and near some elk tracks below it. The elk tracks stopped at these divots and seemed to either blend into the gravel rock, turn back in a 180 to where they came from, or vanish.

I grabbed my camera and told Darrell, "We're filming and we're not leaving for a while." He said, "Why? What do ya mean? Holy Crap, are those Dolly Parton's boobs in the mud?" We both laughed and I used my camera as a magnifier and zoomed the 4k lens deep into the two fresh divots. It was hard to see what they looked like, but because of the proximity to the elk tracks, I was curious as to what this animal was that made them. Yes, it was abundantly obvious it was flesh, bone, and hair that made these, and it seemed to show physiology. One divot was incredibly pristine with signature anatomy, while the other had a crumbled couple of clay clods fall into it. We bent down and began to further examine the scene. "Whatever it is, it ain't no deer or elk," said Darrell confidently. I asked, "Darrell, are these knee impressions?" He said, "It sure looks like a kneecap." We looked down to see the deep hair flow imprinted in the clay of each divot. Beyond we could see small black hairs sticking straight up. It was the equivalent of taking your knuckle and punching it into a wad of clay or play-dough, leaving behind the striations of a person's finger bone, muscle, tendon, and hair. We could kind of rule out a giant knuckle impression and Darrell's joke. Dolly Parton could have never made it up that hill in her heels.

OWL MOON KNEE IMPRESSIONS

Darrell chimed in, "The tree structures I wanted to show ya are up ahead about a quarter-mile. I said to Darrell, "Is this a black bear, elk, cow, or anything he could recognize?" He said, "No I think it's very weird and way too deep and wide...besides that, no ungulate is bending down just on its knees leaving behind a specific right and left divot. I asked, "The hairs, they look fine and small like human type hair." Darrell agreed as we stood there calculating just how fresh this print was. I had The London Tracks in my head as I stared down with my camera rolling. "We can't not cast these, but I need to get supplies and come back," I said. Darrell agreed and we left.

We came back to his house and phoned one of the original crew of the London casting team. The voice on the other end said, "When you cast it, use the entire bag of plaster on the entire impression as a unit." I agreed and told Darrell we needed to come back to document the scene. Darrell is a devoted husband and takes hubby of the year for being there for his wife. Although Darrell was retired, Cindy was working a full-time job as an addiction/PTSD specialist. She had to commute over an hour to and from work five days a week and Darrell always had dinner waiting for her by 5 pm. It was now 4 pm and we had to drive back and get him in the kitchen. There was no way we could document it without our gear anyway and I had to buy some hydro-cal or Fix-it-all patching compound. Darrell and I left the scene and I secured our gear from anywhere that was still open to the public, including the Dollar Tree. Hey, you'd be surprised what kind of tools I got. We met back around 7 pm and all drove up the hill as the moon rose.

As we set up the scene, I gave the camera to Cindy for documentation while Darrell and I measured and collected hairs. I should mention that around this same time I'd started a live podcast, and was dreaming up and looking for content to air. My thought was, who cared if it came back as an ungulate or known mammal. It was an exercise in field collection and it would make great content for an audience. I was never thinking beyond documenting a mystery, and I knew because of the shifting opinion of The London Tracks that this one would be treated with hesitancy. I treated it like it was a rare impression, but considered the outcome to be explainable. We meticulously collected the hair and cast the impressions as a single casting. Cindy was even taken aback by it all and thought it was worthy of casting. At one point the Full Owl Moonrise shone its white light down on us. We then heard from somewhere off in the distance what sounded like a typical Sasquatch howl smothered by a pack of eager coyotes. They sounded far off and had a long siren quality. We would stop periodically and turn to face the sounds coming from the direction of the hills around Cottage Grove Lake.

OWL MOON KNEE & HAIR COLLECTION

Once the impressions had dried we began the tedious task of pulling them up. The impressions were moved from the clay bank and slow slide into the back cab of Darrell's pickup. Surprisingly they were never damaged as they slightly bounced and bobbed down the gravel road back to the Adams family home. We set them in the garage that evening and locked them up. They would need a couple of weeks of complete drying before we revealed any more details from them.

I drove out to Darrell's after work and looked in his garage. I could only see bits of white plaster underneath the now dried and brittle red clay. Once we got close, I could see there were areas ready to reveal the plaster copy. I gloved up and picked off a chunk of red clay like a scab. As I pulled it back with Darrell watching closely, we could both see the rich details exposing themselves. Obvious hair flow and actual individual black hairs poked out. It was soon after that I sent the photos with a letter attached to researcher Cindy Dosen of *The Hominid Enigma Project*. She is, or was, associated with the Sasquatch Olympic Project of Washington State. She is known as a trusted resource with a veterinary background. Her specialty is magnifying and identifying hair samples and trying to match hairs to a specifically known mammal. She agreed to help if I could have them sent to her for study. I agreed and in total, she got one and a half hairs. One with a full root and tip and one with just a tip. I asked her that when the findings came back, would she mind doing me a favor as to speaking about the data.

My podcast Strange Bräu Radio was just starting, and I have a version of it I do live once a month. She said, "Are you sure you don't want to know as soon as I find the culprit?" I said, "Cindy, it doesn't matter, it's all about the process and showing a mystery unfold however it's meant to be." I wanted to do it this way as an outright public act of transparency, and to show that it's ok if you're wrong. Hell, even if you're certain you're right at the time, it's still better to show why you felt that way and learn from it.

The day came on a Sunday in May 2018 for the live podcast to announce what we'd discovered. We brought the impressions in for the live audience to look at and set them on the stage. I brought in Cindy Dosen via our video conference feed and projected her on the big screen. Ron Morehead, author of Quantum Bigfoot was in the audience, along with his wife Keri Campbell. Cindy Dosen was very matter of fact and said, "After a full review I can tell you the hairs you sent me are of no known or classified mammal." She also said the hairs were from extremities in their last stages of resting growth and no postmortem banding was present. In Cindy's estimation, it was a match for another collected Sasquatch hair found in Ocean Shores, Washington, by researcher Scott Taylor. Cindy Dosen also mentioned the hair was only the seventh to match a suspected Sasquatch hair of over two hundred hairs sent to her over the years.

HOMINID ENIGMA REPORT CINDY DOSEN

The completed report was shocking to hear and read. We had backchannel conversations regarding the whole report and just how significant it all could be. I wanted to believe Cindy was correct on her analysis but needed to know what others thought as well. Little did I know how difficult it would be to get more eyes on the evidence. Part of that was word of mouth regarding who found the suggested knees and hairs. Perhaps it was all my earlier talk about Sasquatch not being dominated by known science. A sticky subject for most who only want to see the proof under a microscope or in other predictable ways. I simply was not there, even before this news about the hair, but the coming days, months, and years would only prove to exacerbate my name as a refuge for the bizarre.

Researcher Scott Taylor, who's employed as a lead manager engineer at Boeing Aerospace helped us acquire a simple formulation for weight measurements based on my knee impression in the same soil. Taylor, as mentioned before, was no stranger to skeptics checking his work as a Sasquatch investigator. He's a brilliant man and has come to similar conclusions as to the exotic nature of Sasquatch's behavior. He agreed to assist with our inquiry and told us how to devise a plan for the total weight volume of the impressions. After we concluded a full day of casting my own knees in varying different stages of ambulation, we sent the measurements of my knee vs the Owl Moon Impressions. After a couple of days of emails and calculations, Taylor sent me the final approximate weight of the individual that left the knees. It was a whopping 1200 lbs., plus or minus a couple of hundred lbs. Taylor triple-checked his numbers and so did we. He called me back and said, "I think it's closer to 1400 lbs." I asked if that was merely inertia throwing a blanket of enforcement at the substrate or if that was the actual weight of the individual?" He said, "I think it shows it was most definitely, at the very least, a 1200 lbs. individual." The average weight of the North American Bison is between 1k-2k lbs. An elk weighs in at its heaviest at 800 lbs. and a bull cow somewhere between 1500-2400 lbs. So in a garage, they sat, protected by only a $5.00 tarp.

Two years later, in the spring of 2020, the casted impressions were further analyzed by a Washington State Sonographer, Joe Dragoo. A

Sonographer, unlike an X-Ray tech, uses ultrasound to look at 3-D images of tendons, muscles, and other aspects of human anatomy. Dragoo felt confident that if the impressions were knee prints, and the plaster casts we secured were good enough, he could make a medical determination. He also believed he could further elaborate on the weight it would take to make this impression and the possible range of motion the subject was in. I again warned Dragoo, seeing he had an accredited name, that I am looking into all aspects of the phenomena. This would include the concept of a physical subject leaving the impressions and simply disappearing into thin air. Dragoo assured me he can write a report and just let the medical facts stand on their own. In addition, Scott Taylor, who did the original weight displacement measurements, agreed to weigh in on the Dragoo calculations. The three of us met online a couple of times via video conferencing and mapped out the format of the Dragoo Report concerning The Owl Moon Impressions.

DRAGOO/TAYLOR PAPER

Looking back now to the time shortly after we cast The Owl Moon Impressions, which I can easily do on archived video, there wasn't much more we could do, except for one thing Eryn reminded me of. After we came home and told everyone about the find, she asked me if I left anything? "Left anything, like what?" I asked. She went on to explain how she believed nature was a mirror and that you must leave something after you take something. This was how she lived and dealt with what she called *elementals* or *forest spirits* that dwell here and beyond. I was unfamiliar with the process, but it sounded like a form of mystic interaction and appropriate for the setting. I went back the next day after we set the casting away and left a single hair under a pile of the familiar red dirt. Oddly enough, after we snooped around the area a month later with a Sasquatch researcher Randy Silvey, I found a broken piece of plaster with a long black hair attached to it. I walked over to Randy and handed it to him, "Here dude, take it home and make your kids smile."

4

GREATEST HITS

I t wasn't too long after the suspected knees arrived back at the house that Darrell and Cindy both heard strange sounds around their property. Most of these sounds would come at night, but they were also heard at all hours of the day. I would get equally random instant messages while at work about the latest strange noises.

On one of the first occasions, I was told that while Darrell was asleep they would hear footsteps below them in the house. They thought someone or something had unlocked the downstairs deadbolt and wandered in from one side of the house and up the stairs. I reminded him that the area may connect to the early settlers who once called this land home and that perhaps it was what they call a "stone tape," a theory that supernatural sounds and apparitions are a residual form of noise that recycles itself on a sort of psychic loop.

They would hear things not only in their house walking about, but the familiar sound of objects sliding on counters or doors creaking open. When sleeping beside the upstairs window they may hear distant yells or what sounded like someone or something walking over the 4-foot-tall metal gates and slapping or tapping the side of the house.

It's not uncommon for EESIs to report such sounds. Often, house slapping or hitting is a key sign a Sasquatch is nearby and is perhaps trying to persuade the property owner to come outside to initiate more direct interaction. Darrell did go outside with his small dog Izzy. He would wait for the dog to relieve itself while he investigated the after-hours noises. Most of the time nothing seemed out of the ordinary, but occasionally Darrell would describe the hair on his arms and neck rising like a static charge was in the air. Izzy would remain curious and observant, but rarely appear scared.

The smaller tap or larger HIT sounds were to be the beginning of learning more about the property. These "hit" sounds were small or giant pops that seem directed mainly at the South area of the house. It was described as something throwing a stone at high speeds and hitting a target with a loud pop or hit. I suggested we record audio in separate areas of the property. Darrell agreed and we devised a plan to record in two separate areas. We would do so as much as we could, but especially when the sun went down.

My go-to recorder for audio collecting is the Tascam DR-05 stereo recorder. Previously, I'd only used this recorder for witness descriptions of previous sightings. I rarely had access to an area where constant activity was being reported, let alone sounds that were worthy of review. I was also untrained in an adequate way to download the audio for review. If you're going to record consistently, your review has to be just as consistent. Imagine recording for ten hours every night, you would have to listen to all ten hours for these unpredictable and fleeting sounds. There had to be a better way, and there was. I just didn't use it yet.

Darrell would record with his Sony Digital Dictaphone, which he hooked up to his parabolic dish. He would position his recorder in the backyard and simply strap the arm of the parabolic dish using cheap package tape to an old wooden kitchen chair. He would then point the dish to the abandoned apple orchard, which was shadowed over from a large, wooded hillside beside a major power line. My recorder would usually be set up outside the property near the front porch.

As time persisted over the first couple of weeks of recording, so did the sounds. I would often put on headphones and listen to the evening sounds while driving my semi-truck. Larger stretches of highway allow you to listen to long segments of audio, however boring most of it was. When you would hear it for yourself, your mind would race to debunk it. However, one thing caught my attention regarding the more benign HIT sounds - there was no secondary drop heard. To explain, if it was a projectile being thrown, you would never hear the object hit the ground. However, the roar of my diesel engine would drown out audio clips Darrell would send to me whilst driving. It would take me going back to his home and uploading the sounds so I could listen to them through good headphones. There are programs one can download to help further with an audio review. I had only messed around with other pieces of software that could help isolate audio visually, but not enough to say I knew what I was doing.

TAPS, SLAPS, AND HITS

After work one evening I drove back out to Darrell's, who would often just upload the sounds to his computer and listen through the whole raw audio using his computer speakers. It was like a needle in the haystack if you didn't have a time stamp on when the sound occurred, if you even heard it. While sitting outside the house with Darrell, we talked about a free program you could download called Audacity, which would allow us to see the audio as we listened to it. It's the equivalent of watching even the most minute sounds stream like a sonar wave on your very own computer screen. This would give us the bonus of reviewing quickly as we fast-forwarded the audio to sounds we could see that looked important to hear, isolate and save. If we were both to become familiar with Audacity then we could knock out daily reviews in only an hour.

Darrell then brought up something strange he and Cindy noticed in the house. It was in the downstairs guest bedroom by the computer. He said it looked like a weird child's handprint that was smeared to a plywood door. I asked to check it out and we walked inside to the nearby bedroom. Darrell closed the door behind me and pointed down at one of the strangest looking handprints I had ever seen.

5
_____

CHUCKY'S ROOM

We both kneeled to inspect on camera these small chalky white handprints that were depressed up against the veneer of the door. It was very childlike in one way, but also gnarled like a deformity in another. They were small, if it were a child, I would say the child would have to be about 5-7 years of age. Each finger was separated unnaturally, at least to my eye, like they were spread open in the web by extra skin. Also, each finger looked flexible as though made of rubber. They bent inward unnaturally as they spread open like someone was pushing their way out or leaning up against something. There was no discernible thumbprint, only a small fleck of white where the thumb could have set down, but each small, weird handprint was only four fingers. That's when Darrell said, "It looks like Chucky the Doll was in here or something." I laughed nervously and grabbed my camera, but remembered I had a UV flashlight in my pack out in the car. I always tried to have a "go-pack" in my trunk whenever I could. I ran back with my camera running and told Darrell we are going to turn off the lights now. He flipped the switch and I turned on the blacklight.

CHUCKY'S ROOM

The handprint glowed with a phosphorous purple hue. It highlighted so much more detail not present in the initial scan over the latent white print. You could not see a fingerprint, but you could see where some of the finger pads appeared to rest, not to mention the palm. If you pulled the blacklight away, all that would remain was this chalky white oily substance adhered to the cheap factory door. It was like someone took a rubber doll's hand, dipped it in water-based paint mixed with grease, and slammed it against the door. Again, no discernible trace of a thumb on either hand. I asked Darrell if we could try one more thing with this impression. He asked what I had in mind. I suggested we need to document for keeps and dust it. Although I didn't have a fingerprint lifting kit with me, I had watched a couple of researchers dust for Sasquatch prints before and had a good idea how it was done.

We decided we would do it and used what we had around the house. I also ran to the department store and bought a piece of foam core board, black chalk, and looked for a large makeup brush. I couldn't find one and searched the store for something comparable. Cindy might have had one at home, so I ran back with what I could find. It turns out there was no useful makeup brush around to collect the handprints so we crushed up a charcoal pencil until it was a fine powder. We poured the black powder atop an old paper bag and then used the only thing we had around. It turns out Darrell had been given a bunch of peacock feathers from a nearby farmer. It was with these delicate peacock feathers that we dusted over the strange handprints before transferring them to the back in packaging tape. Then we simply pulled the tape back and adhered it to a piece of white core bored. Once we transferred the dusted black handprints to the clear tape and placed it flush against the pristine white surface, we could see just how bizarre these four-fingered small hands were.

Was it possible the previous owners had a child young with a birth defect that could have done this? Yes, but that means Darrell and Cindy had never seen the handprints before buying it. Also, the prints were chalky white. What would be on the hands of a four-fingered child that looked like paint? We didn't swab for a biological.

About nine months after dusting and collecting the prints I would attend a conference with them in tow. The conference, held in Ocean Shores, Washington, was an annual event that brought speakers from around the world to discuss researched evidence of the Paranormal. Included in that 2019 speaker roster was UFO researcher Derrel Simms. Simms, also nicknamed the *Alien Hunter*, had an extensive career as an author of books dedicated to non-human abduction and alien implantation. It was of Simms's opinion that these abductions and surgical implants had certain patterns surrounding them. One of these patterns was the findings of small and large four-fingered oily handprints that had been infused or even apparently burned into the victims. This could be on the skin, clothing, and anywhere on the surface of whatever they touched. I showed Simms the copy of the handprints we had secured, and his eyes grew interested. He agreed with me they seemed off for a human and the fact the thumb was not visible, held a particular interest. We discussed over a cup of coffee some particulars of what my findings were, and he shared his shadowy background with me, some of which I already knew from following his work before our meeting.

Chucky's Room would have to wait, and the still present handprints that were seemingly permanently stuck to the door.

CHUCKY DUSTING

6

BUILDING BIGGY

What seemed like a lifetime ago I was a product design major at the University of Oregon. I worked as a technical theater major with an emphasis on production design. It was there I studied for about 18 months learning how to build props. In my head, I was always building a Sasquatch model and thinking about how it might look on display. I had attempted at Ike's pizza to create one for our monthly meetings, but he was not impressive as far as accuracy from witness reports. If I ever made another one, I would need a large space to design him. As luck would have it, Darrell would end up finishing the large metal shop on his property and offering the space to me for storage and a Sasquatch build. So I came up with a reason to build one and a date was set for me to finish. The concept was simple, build an 8-foot-tall Sasquatch in honor of Ron Morehead's Sierra Sasquatch sighting of the 1970s. I would then invite fans of Ron to come with us up to the mountains where we'd premier Biggy in the forest for a recreation of the Sierra Camp. There they could have breakfast, get their photograph with him, and spend an evening back at Darrell's for a BBQ. I had three months to pull it off and it would take every bit of that to complete.

One day in May I brought via my Jeep a large block of Styrofoam to carve. After setting it out back at Darrell's he suggested that my trips to and from his house should turn into a full-time living on site. I would bring my trailer down to his home and build after work, often all weekend. I agreed and thanked him for the rent-free option. It was only a couple of weeks after he suggested it that I moved in and parked my trailer under a shaded tree near an overgrown artisan spring. It was perfect for the time, and I made no plans to leave until a was finished. Every day was a different mode of construction and to boot, I was in a prime area for actual backyard Sasquatch reports. The knees, after all, were found less than twenty miles away and there were recent encounters up the road. If we had time then we would examine the actual plaster impressions of the knees and collect as much hair from the scene as possible.

My son would come over after school and hang out with me sometimes. There was not much for a sixteen-year-old to do once there if they were not into collecting hair samples, so that's what we did. He would glove and mask up with a pair of tweezers and slowly separate mud from plaster. We built a small archeology kit for them fashioned out of a retooled soft-bristled toothbrush and a rubber dental pick. He would assist in the overall design of Biggy while helping to look for possible Sasquatch hair embedded in the plaster knees. The hair of a Sasquatch structure is important and rarely done properly. If I had the time and tools I would hand ream actual acrylic salon hair weaves to fiberglass and foam, but this would take way too long. I ended up finding an FX shop near Paramount Studios in LA that dealt with large reams of 4-inch-long acrylic hair by the yard. It was fairly costly, so I made sure my measurements were only slightly over what I needed.

Later that week the yardage of acrylic hair arrived and was rolled out on the newly poured cement floor. It reached almost from one side of the garage to the next. It put the build into perspective for everyone as we could see just how much hair would be needed for a structure of around 8-foot. To get the hair to stick to the structure on this scale, I would have to carefully make a pattern out of butcher paper, as our grandparents probably did for clothes years back. I wanted to act like I knew what I was doing from years of experience, but like so many things in my life...I jumped in head first and taught myself how to erect a Sasquatch.

Soon the fiberglass and resin would be formed over the patterned foam muscle flow. This would not only make Biggy durable but light enough to carry from one venue to another. There was a deadline to finish him by fall of 2018, but for the most part, I took my time and worked on him between sleeping, working, and studying the suspected knee impressions.

The concept was coming to life, and I am sure Darrell and Cindy must have wondered a time or two just what they had invited to their home. I made sure to always keep organized and tidy in my borrowed monster workshop, which is kind of ironic considering I was building an oversized Sasquatch at their home, or what Darrell and I were calling "Frankenstein's Lab." It's impossible to say for certain if building Biggy there was the reason for the events about to unfold, or if bringing the plaster knees down from the mountain was the catalyst. Regardless, "The Lab" was about to show its repeatable power and invite us into a world of impossible experiments.

7

GIFTING BEGINS

Trout season in Cottage Grove Lake usually starts around the third week of April. I invited Darrell and my son to hop in my boat and spend the morning and afternoon fishing. This was the same lake the London Tracks were cast from, and I had never taken my boat there. It seemed fitting to have Jude float over the mudflats where his quick sense of interest reported the prints back in 2012. We spent the afternoon looking for clever ways for me to get my hook snagged in swamp grass and for the most part we had a lot of laughs and zero bites. It wasn't until we got back to Darrell's that the real catch of the day would be found.

We unhitched the boat and noted near the steps of my trailer a single orange and yellow bobber in the gravel. I turned to Darrell and said, "Did you lose this, dude?" He assured me he didn't even have any bobbers, let alone one that looks like that. It was completely in reason to drop the fishing supplies in haste on our way out to the lake. We did not make much of it and set it in the boat for later use.

BOBBER

It was only about a week after that when I walked into the shop and found something oddly placed on the counter near a roll of duct tape. It was a small plastic blue dinosaur standing perfectly on the table facing forward. Darrell had recently had family over and perhaps it was the children who might have left the toy. I went up to the front door while Darrell and Cindy were having dinner. It was common for them to eat meals at set times and they often invite me in for dinner with them. I was invited in and showed them the toy. They said, "Where did ya find that?" I told them exactly. Darrell said, "I was just in there and there was nothing like that only a couple of hours ago." He and Cindy assured me the company that left had no toys like that and it would be impossible for Darrell to miss it. Again, we played it off as something innocuous and just weird. Perhaps not even linked to the bobber. However, Darrell said, "ya know I did find something weird myself the other day while I was out hiking near the Owl Moon Prints". He went on to say he and his dog went on a day hike up a single marked trail. As they walked into the woods, they noted how thirsty they both were, and the lack of immediate water nearby. On their way back to the truck to get home for a drink, they saw a bright red thermos in the middle of the trail they had just walked in on. It was standing up and dead center, which was impossible to miss on the single trail in. He walked me into the garage and showed me what he felt was left for him. Immediately, it reminded me of the blue suede shoes. It was placed in a spot where it would be noticed right after the person was just there. It was standing right side up and presented with age and wear. It also had a mossy patina attached to the lid. Lastly, it could have been a response to a need. Darrell's dog was thirsty, after all, and that was the perfect container to hold fluids. I could see Darrell was struggling with this theory, and in all honesty, I was as well.

The Native Americans tell of stories living beside Sasquatch and even trading with them. Stories of smoked salmon being traded for this or that by Natives to the Sasquatch. I even took testimony from a case up at the Chehalis Tribe Reservation from a fella who said his grandma would trade out fish for needed household items. I thought at the time it was folklore with the possibility of weirdness for sure, but this was not what I expected. However, we never saw Sasquatch place these items, whatever was happening loved to keep us guessing.

With each strange sound we recorded, generally, we would find a new item or gift. The gifts that were left became overwhelming in frequency, location, and connection to us. If we spoke about something on the property, we learned the property was listening. It wouldn't matter how soft you spoke or what you spoke about, the fact was that some items left were associated with things we had just spoken of. Not only were items left regularly, but there were also disturbances, property damage, stick glyphs, handprints, hair and footprints.

1. Bobber | gravel driveway
2. Thermos | middle of trail above the house
3. Plastic toy dinosaur | on work shelf in a locked shop
4. Small, burned Balsa wood | 7 feet up on the right side of the vinyl awning of camper
5. Small carnelian agate | 7 feet up on the right side of the vinyl awning of camper
6. Large walking stick | upright leaning on camper door next to a similar stick I found.
7. Small toothbrush | taken from toolbox in locked shop and set on plaster knee impression
8. Three deep vertical grouped 12-inch scratches in gravel | front door to camper

9. Four small dents to aluminum camper | backside facing the tree-line

10. Guest bedroom screen pinched, and hole poked | main house lower floor

11. Three large rocks placed in a triangle formation | roof of Darrell's pickup truck

12. Small rubber goldfish | atop a flat rock I left out behind my trailer

13. Small chunk of petrified wood | Inside my locked trailer, placed in the sink

14. Baseball sized rock | Darrell's locked house, found dead center on the living room floor

15. Large chewed stick | shoved 4 feet up into the vent of Darrell's outdoor AC unit

16. Large crystals | placed in a cleared off circle in the gravel drive

17. Baseball | placed deep on a mound of gravel behind Darrell's pick-up

18. Chocolate Opal | found near an outdoor **parabolic** in the backyard

19. Small/Large chunks of conglomerate rock | usually placed near the shop wall

20. Huge urine streaks | in line with the camper extension cord some 3x2 feet in size

RANDOM AND TAILORED GIFTS

Most, if not all these items had some wear to them, especially the manmade ones. They reminded me of things forgotten at a campsite, overlooked while someone packed out from their stay. Each item had been used or broken off something, each with a weathered patina with dirt in the creases and moss growing off in some cases. I couldn't help but think of the sneakers left for the kid. It seemed like a repeatable behavior and one willing to go the extra mile for providing us with whatever we mentioned.

By the end of June 2018, we had several examples of anomalous gifting and disturbances. We tried to account for as much of it as we could be recording everything. This was mainly done with an accurate time and date stamp via a smartphone camera. However, there was so much activity we could not always keep up with it and God knows what we missed when we weren't looking. I was forced to work long hours as a truck driver and Darrell, although he was home, did not know of the potential score he was sitting on. I call it a score because after ten years this was the culmination. I quickly guessed and clued into what was most likely visiting and begged Darrell to keep track of everything while I was away. I was manic and obsessive in tone when I asked and a bit much for anyone. Darrell is too nice to say, but he must have thought I was bonkers, I sure would have. I warned him again, "Things are about to get wild around here man, and your public friendship with me in the Sasquatch world of Relic Hominid bullshit won't do ya any favors." He would laugh and pretend he didn't care about that kind of stuff. I didn't buy it. It hurts when you respect someone's work, and they look at ya as a fool." I guess I warned him as best I could and let the chips fall.

From later April to October 2018, the events would come almost every day with little to no break. Most of it you couldn't ignore, however, some of them seemed to be placed in areas where it was meant to be found at a specific weird time. This was amplified when we would guess the gifting, timing, and placement. In those moments, it was almost a throw down and an even more spectacular gift would appear. It was almost as if they were saying, "Ya you two, of course, it was me!"

Darrell's wife, Cindy Adams, would mostly stand back from our initial inquiry and poke holes in our theories. I suppose it was Cindy I was most concerned about finding my presence erratic. However, Darrell was recently retired and home alone with little to no schedule. She was working forty hours a week and commuting over thirty minutes each way. I think she saw me as a sort of answer to her hubby getting depressed with his newfound freedom. It was isolating to be that far away from any family or friends. Besides me around, it was mainly Darrell and his dog Izzy. So Cindy and I would talk about what my experience was and what I suspected was occurring. She would often ask me, "What are you going to do with all this stuff?" It was the same question the family was asking me. I had no clue as to how to answer that question because I never intended to only collect data. I was more interested in where this would lead me and what I would be shown. I was challenged to keep my opinions to myself and politely, I said, "I will write a book about it someday and share it." Cindy then would ask Darrell and me to challenge the supposed Sasquatch like a genie in a bottle. "If it's so in tune with us and brings us magic goodies, why doesn't it bring me a bag of money?" We laughed on the porch as she spoke the words and never thought much of her request.

It wasn't more than four or five days later that I found a brand new zipped freezer bag set down in an area where I'd secretly placed an antique mailbox. It was there I would hide things inside, raise the flag and wait and see what happened. This is where I found the red bag set right in front of the mailbox, hidden under the blackberry thorns. The spot was only about 50 yards away from the front of the house but concealed enough that Darrell didn't even see it. I grabbed the bag and unzipped it. The clean white plastic coating sewn inside the bag was pristine and had no wear and tear in the slightest. It looked like it was taken directly from the factory it was shipped from. These are the bags you would bring to a grocery store and keep cold items for a long commute back home. At the bottom of the bag are three barely ripe blackberries. They are grouped in a corner and nothing else. They left no stain on the white plastic and must have been freshly plucked from the now budding and producing vines. I brought the bag of three berries to Cindy and said, "I don't know if a bank will cash them, but maybe you can make a small pie." It was our first dent in Cindy's armor, yet she persisted with possible doubt, especially when it came to the idea of a being reading minds.

There was a momentum occurring and we needed to stay focused on communication. I checked with other folks online to seek advice from people that had dealt with areas like this to a degree greater than myself. Something more than Sasquatch was occurring and we had to be prepared for impossible scenarios. I called Eryn up and talked to her about the events and she would listen, but I could tell it was laced with concern. I tried to relay to her I was managing the balance between work, my son, and the Adams Family, but she knew I was not. It was all I was talking about and nothing else came first, nothing. I would later find out that she was concerned enough to walk away from me as I lurched down the abyss. There was grooming going on by an unseen force and I was taking its hand and being guided. Each time there was an experience, it was impossible and supernatural. It was like a God interacting with me, so it was more personal than my experience with Christ. The harsh truth is I had no evidence of a Christian God or any God except creation. This force was a daily walk and exhibiting abilities beyond what was witnessed by me or others in any ninety-minute Sunday church scene. Certainly, I could never discuss this with a person of faith, they would only call it demonic. I became secluded in my thoughts as we approached the phenomena.

The Adams allowed me to soak in the miracle of their home and share as much of it as I wanted, however I wanted. From the beginning, they insisted on using their real names and even mentioned where they lived. I argued against that, but I intended to respect their wishes and be a guest to their "guest." When my schedule would allow, I would turn up at all hours and walk the property freely. I was even given a key and invited to dinner, whatever, and whenever!

Everything that I owned was on that land in 2018. I had it all parked in about 40 square feet near the new shop Darrell just built. My trailer was 15 feet away from my Jeep's parking spot and my boat another 15-inch behind my Jeep. It was in these areas I would receive items. It would periodically take me some time to find the objects or signs, but eventually, I would. The boat was a 14-foot aluminum fishing boat with bench seats, trolling motor, and two oars. The Jeep was a 2007 Jeep Commander in perfect condition. My camper was a 16-foot second-hand camper with single bed, bath, and kitchen. The true bachelor life of a gypsy who had what he carried on his back. It was a relief after two painful divorces and living this way, it felt like I had the wind at my back. Eryn would often use the quote, "Let's you and I slip the leash." I fell in love with her when she would talk that way. I slipped the leash and was living in a true mystery.

The gifts or objects of significance would arrive at all hours of the day. It didn't matter where you were or what time it was. You would turn around and there would be something new. A moment that stands out has to be when my boat became a gift basket of sorts for a couple of amazing treasures. I was having technical problems with my smartphone. I mentioned the technical issue I was having while at the property and also while on the road with Darrell. One day, while snooping around for a sign, I looked in my boat and under the right side, hidden under my wooden oar, was a muddy cell phone. It was broken, old, and looked like it was found on a lakebed or mud bog, a sidekick flip phone to be exact. We tried to operate and charge it to see who it belonged to, but it was toast. How could I have not linked the two events? How could a phone hide under my boat oar?

Another event happened in the boat, which I believe had something to do with my son and me. Around July or August of 2018, he'd recently moved and wanted to set up his new computer room with decorative lights. He decided what was better than a Christmas tree with lights and decorations on it. I guess he wanted to celebrate early, and who are we to say you're a tad early, son? I did the same and hung my outdoor lights atop my camper awning. We shared a couple photos of our early Christmas spirit and had a chuckle. I had no idea that our early decorating efforts would inspire a move from the phenomena. I would now check the boat inside and out to see if more items would appear and that is when, under the same oar as before, I found an antique glass Christmas ball. It was painted red, green, and gold with a small carved holly leaf on top. I debated whether to tell my son about this and told his mother instead. She looked it over on the cell phone and said she recognized it and that it appeared to be one from her collection. My son was over thirty miles away and there was no way he or my ex could find the Adams and sneak it in my boat. They didn't even know about the cell phone, so how would they know where I would look. It was adding up to be way stranger than Sasquatch. It seemed tailor-made for individuals. It knew me and my friends and family. It knew where I was and what I was speaking about. It knew where to have me look. It knew how to size me up. It was something so personalized and magical it stole the focus from anything and everything else. The Tailor Effect would go on to be how I would explain the phenomena of The Owl Moon Lab.

The interactions became even more extreme and a sense of humor, or joking tone, was noted by all of us. This is a common thread with Extended Experiences of Sasquatch or Paranormal Interaction. The Tailor's comedic timing is impeccable.

Cindy asked for a chunk of gold. She would say these comments flippantly and with sarcasm, as if. Right on time, a few days later, I get home and visit with Darrell in the garage, still in the construction process of building Biggy. Darrell sees something atop of my trailer awning and says, "Did you see that when you pulled in?" We had grown accustomed to seeing gifts put on my trailer canopy awning, but this was a new one for sure. We both walk up and grab the camera.

I step under the awning and cascade the item off the top so it would slide down to Darrell, who was waiting. I couldn't believe it, in his hands was a bright hunk of something gold. It wasn't what Cindy asked for, but it sure was rare. It turned out to be a brass rifle shell. The worn-out company logo wears thin at the base of the shell, but Darrell made out the word Peter's. This is well-known ammo, primarily known for the Winchester 308 rifle round. Again, this gift had a familiar patina on it and was placed sometime during the day.

CHRISTMAS BALL AND GOLDEN GIFTS

To bring the point home, this was not a hoaxer listening twenty-four seven and sneaking up on us. Remember, we left out audio and cameras, though we were mostly reliant on audio after finding the cameras malfunctioned or only showed odd image anomalies. Whoever or whatever this was leaving gifts was not in love with the idea of cameras hidden all over. Usually, motion sensor lights are a good way to get rid of interaction, or limit it, however, the audio recording was never an issue. So we went for interaction on their terms and to not overtly stash or hide anything from them.

8

TRICKSTER & TAILOR

Throughout history, you will find oral and written traditions regarding The Trickster. It is in the story of The Trickster you will find attributes of what for the most part is gameplay or mysterious interaction with an unknown being. It will toy with you and in the end, drive you mad if you let it. There are elements of this to Sasquatch interaction and people that are lucky enough, in my estimation, to be extended experiencers of Sasquatch interaction or EESIs usually get the brunt of The Trickster. I saw it for certain in the people I interviewed over the last ten years. What is not talked about is the spell it can put you under as the interaction is taking place. There is a type of immediate omniscience to their direct communicating with individuals. These individuals can feel unique, chosen, or special. This is where things get complicated.

The Trickster is like The Tailor, it is a better name for the interaction most EESIs describe. How does The Trickster become The Tailor? It does so by having the schematics or blueprints of individuals. The same way a tailor may take measurements to design a perfectly fitted suit or dress, this is how the Owl Moon tailor worked. For example, in looking back at the blue suede shoe story we see a perfect example of this. A specific person is chosen at a specific time and place. The tailor awaits a perfect moment where this individual is alone and heading to a specific spot where these custom gifted objects are waiting to be found, Tailor-made. The same could be said for the necklace on the boot, the muddy cell phone, and the brass shell.

EESIs are often blamed for being self-absorbed whack jobs that feel Sasquatch has chosen them as individuals to work with or even through. This makes it damn near impossible for the "Aper" community to sit in the same room with these folks that embrace the woo, or in this case The Tailor. Sometimes I can understand why It sounds as though instead of carefully collected information on Sasquatch habituations, these weirdos are just making up stories to get their fifteen minutes. Of course, they are right, there are those people out there who are like that, but generally, I found it was usually not the EESI. It usually was some self-prescribed expert of the great outdoors who has definitive proof via advanced tech deployment. It makes sense that most EESIs would not be seeking glory or fame. They, for the most part, are separated from the expected social norms and live generally where fewer people do. EESIs who deal with this for years grow weary of trying to prove anything to anyone based upon the severity of The Tailor's supernatural omniscience. Just like Santa Clause, it sees you when you're sleeping, and it knows when you're awake. Even better, does it know when you've been bad or good and does The Tailor have values that dictate what bad and good even are? I tend to think it does, for the most part, at least the ones we were getting to know at The Lab. It seemed too playful and meaningful in the beginning and had almost a juvenile air about it.

I made a call to an EESI out in Montana about certain behaviors exhibited by the phenomena at The Lab. They heard the story and agreed there was a younger type of energy playing with us and in her mind, it was juvenile Sasquatch coming to the property. She said that we need to make sure they know you are appreciative of their presence but you gotta put more walls up. I asked, "How do you do that?" She mentioned how she does it at her own home. "In my case, I am the den-mother of the fraternity, and these are my frat boys." I let them

know what is allowed and what is not, and they listen. If they don't
listen, I put lights or cameras on for a while, and they stay back." I
assured her it was not just Sasquatch around this area and there was a
Star Wars bar scene happening here. We were getting all sorts of what
seemed like ghost or UFO-type interaction and they seemed anything
but juvenile. I took her words to heed, and it wasn't too long before I
needed them.

Now, living at the property, I studied the house and land daily. I
examined the way the gravel carport looked and would walk the area
looking for signature footprints. I would study the house windows at a
certain angle in the light to see if skin or hair smudges would be left. I
was looking around for things moved or gifted. However, we were not
expecting property damage, and this was very noticeable.

It started off with what appeared to be a rip on the outside window
screen of one of the bottom bedrooms. We looked closer and could see
the aluminum flange of the screen was also bent and split. It looked
like someone had poked the screen with their finger, ripped it, and
then tried to pry the window. The bedroom where this happened
would be an important milestone later in understanding just how
strange this place was.

Then we noticed the brand-new rain gutters on the shop were
pinched about 11 feet up. Leading to this newly discovered damage, on
the outer metal wall, was a diagonal streak of dried mud. We didn't
recall it ever being there right after the builders left and went so far as
to even phone the builders and show him photographs of the damage.
He actually was offended by the question and assured me, and
especially Darrell, that he would never leave a job with damage.
Darrell agreed and the question then remained, who or what?

The final straw was when we found the two bent t-posts in the
backyard. The t-posts were used to secure the wire fence that separated
the abandoned apple orchard. They are very secure and strong forged
steel not easily moved or bent. These were both twisted down about
three-quarters of the way up at about 20 percent. I noticed the recorder
had not been checked from the night before and asked Darrell to come
and check the sounds. We fast-forwarded through usual hit and smack

sounds and went looking for something big. That is when I discovered a thirty-second audio clip of what sounded like something stomping up to his backyard and yelling with a strange bark and grumble. It then either crosses through the backyard and over the fence or smacks the fence and walks away in a huff. The audio is telling of a subject moving with purpose towards the house. It reminded me of the T-Rex scene in Jurassic Park when the water ripples, only this was much faster and had no crescendo. It just pops into existence on the audio and erupts with a stomp. We took the advice from our source in Montana and treat the scenario like a frat house out of control.

PROPERTY DAMAGE

That night I walked to the tree line in the back of the house behind the orchard and talked to The Trickster & Tailor. It felt crazy but if I didn't at least try to set boundaries with them then how bad would this get? I said, "Listen, you gotta knock this shit off. You can't just come here and ruin these people's property, accidentally or not. They won't want you here if you keep it up. Ya have to be quiet now or this ain't gunna work out for any of us."

I walked back to the house and thought to myself, what the hell was I doing? I felt like I was nuts at that point and maybe I was seeking council from a nut in Montana who was affecting my judgment. It wasn't the first time I talked to the forest in hopes to see or hear something, but this was a whole new level. I was interacting and taking a stand with an unseen force. It was their move and I had to wait to see what would happen.

The next morning after I got back from another long night on the road, Darrell told me via text what had happened. I was just a little suspect as to what he'd written and wondered if he was seeing things. He told me "the t-posts were now bent back!" I read it at the time I was broken down on the side of the highway in an overheated semi. I didn't have good enough reception at the time to send or receive images or calls so I waited to see for myself. When I got back to The Lab, I hopped out of my Jeep and walked through to the backyard. It was just like he said, someone had bent the t-posts almost back at a vertical angle. I walked up to both of them and noticed one was a better job than the other, but still, it was daylight and less than twenty-four hours after my tree talk. It was moments like this that took hoaxing way off the blamed source. It would have taken someone removing the t-posts hydraulically, mechanically reshaping them and then quickly re-posting them back into the ground without untying the fence. There was no way, and the message was received, we heard you and will play by your rules.

If there's any lesson to understanding The Tailor it's perhaps this. The items and actions taking place on behalf of the EESI are meant for them and not their neighbor. It is a form and function scenario that is useful only as a sign for a specific individual. It seems as though "wearing" this figurative suit fitted only for these individuals out in public is the equivalent of showing off. The Tailor does not like showing off and perhaps that is because of one prevalent quality that overshadows the message, Ego. There is no room for this emotion when working with The Tailor and it will set EESI up for less direct contact in the end. Ego thrives in humans, mainly a man's urge for respect and admiration from his neighbor. The Tailor thrives in anonymity and specific interaction with a human's mental or spiritual state. I had seen far too many men fall down the ego trap feeling they were now, "The Chosen One" and they alone transcribed The Tailor's secret code. It was not just men by any means, a fair amount of women felt they were vibrationally more in tune with phenomena. Men would shout from their own personal Mount Sinai, "I am the true voice of all knowledge on this mystery," while ladies insistently droned on and on about how they feel and what their spirit guides would tell them. Both are insufferable and it's hard for The Tailor to make any proper outfit for these types.

9

GETTING CLOSER

R egular life got in the way of my studying the Owl Moon Lab. Life outside the Lab seemed loathsome and I was immersing myself twenty-four seven into documenting the intensive interaction. For the period of a couple of months, I got by on only a couple hours of sleep a night and would lay awake in my camper with an amplified recorder in my ear or layout by the fire pit in a zero gravity chair. I would hear amazing sounds of things approach, erupt or whisper. Now the farmer up the road could be heard across the field. He would keep odd hours, but the sounds I was interested in were close to the source often less than 30 feet away. One night while I was sleeping, I recorded myself snoring and stirring in the camper around midnight and outside the camper near my recorder, you could hear what sounded like an animal eating. It sounded like whatever it was smacked its lips with wet slurping gulps less than 15 feet away from my camper window while it stripped thorn-covered branches of blackberries. I would try and peek out the window to catch whoever it or whatever it was, but the camper would creak and moan on its springs, and inevitably I could never see much of anything. I was working graveyard and was leaving at prime times for visitations from what I suspected was a Sasquatch individual, however, I was almost always recording with my trusty Tascam DR-05 field recorder. If I were to make any product or tech gear recommendations, this recorder is a true beast at a reasonable price.

One day after getting back from a long haul in Seattle, I came back to the camper and noticed an obvious trail of ripe blackberries strewn about the gravel drive in front of my camper. Under the awning you could see a trail of blackberries, whole and not smooshed, leading out to the tree line.

I called Darrell out once again from the comforts of his air-conditioned house. We followed the trail of blackberries to the exact spot we'd heard something run before. As I looked around for my recorder under the vinyl awning stretched out from my camper, I saw a purple wet spot. The awning is about 7-foot high at the section I could see it splayed, which was far too high for it to be explained by natural elements. The juice was just drying and still had a seed or two attached from the 6-8 inch spray. There were several things I should have done immediately to collect the sample I was staring at, but instead I went straight to the recorder and downloaded that evening's sounds. On the recorder, you can clearly hear something eating and chewing the mic head only a few feet from my camper window. All of a sudden, an immense gurgling wet sneeze erupts on the recording and the smacking of lips continues. Darrell hears the recording alongside me as we stare back at the camper and the purple stain. It was impossible to not create a scenario accompanying the sounds. Something had been standing right beside my camper while I was at work, enjoyed a bounty of fresh blackberries, and then while under my camper awning sneezed and left behind a huge purple stain of berry juice as it left back into the woods. Now was it a Sasquatch? I think so based upon the audio and the way the berries were dropped one by one as it left into the wood line. It does beg the question though, why did it bother exposing itself to eating these blackberries? There were plenty of ways it could have been seen suddenly out front of the trailer and it was recorded. There were thousands of acres of ripe berries all over the forest where nobody could have seen it. However, perhaps it wasn't in a state of full physicality.

BLACKBERRY SNEEZE

Like I explained up at Oz, there was the time when I heard something run up behind me in a clearing in broad daylight and saw nothing. If it was cloaked standing there and a passerby suddenly walked on the scene, would they have witnessed floating berries and the sudden burst of a purple guesser shot upwards onto the undercoating of my awning? Soon enough Darrell would come to believe the latter along with me that yes, whatever was on his property could cloak or go invisible.

10

INVISIBLE

Twice Darrell was privy to seeing something using invisibility to obscure their true identity. He never said he saw a Sasquatch go from skin and bone to cloaked, but he did have a couple of moments where his reality of perception was changed by what he was viewing.

The first time was when he and my son were standing beside the trailer and looking out over the underbrush at something. They both describe this high noontime sighting where there was a tall, pixelated entity watching them. They described it as the movie Predator although to me the shape sounded more like that of a typical Sasquatch. Pixelated cone head, no neck, large wide shoulders, and tall standing in the reeds only 20-feet away in broad daylight. I never saw this but ran to them as they both swear to what they saw. Both have 20/20 vision and are familiar with a heat mirage, it was not that. It simply vanished and nothing more was seen.

The second time was after a night walk on the property and out past the sheepdog farm about a mile away. This night I set up my thermal camera, a FLIR camera system made for an old iPhone I still have. It simply snapped over the power slot and switched the regular phone camera lens into a thermal unit. I had it popped out of the bathroom ceiling vent like a submarine periscope. The visibility was limited but it was enough to rule out cougars, which we eventually caught with it, and any other heat source. It was hidden well enough to catch a hoaxer or prankster. We had kind of ruled out pranks by this point, but it was still in the back of my head as a possibility that sometimes it could all be a practical joke. So we get back from the night walk about an hour after I leave the FLIR running and as we walk back to my trailer I go inside to grab my camera. As I reach around the corner to grab it, the thermal is still filming and all at once I hear something come steamrolling right at Darrell. Whoever it was came running from behind my trailer, past the back of Darrell and dashed away on two legs. I stick my head out the door as Darrell screams, "What the hell!" All we hear is the sound of it leaving on the gravel and then jumping into the dry leaves and brush off the side of the drive. It was massive, lightning quick, and very similar to the Oz event, which isn't easily explainable. The thermal unit sat useless in my shaking hand as I looked at Darrell like we'd just seen a ghost, when in a way we had.

Stories of cloaking or invisibility may be the way The Tailor persuades you to think something is not there when it actually is. Perhaps it plays with your mind then plays with bending light or diving into portals. In all of my experiences, I never saw direct evidence of cloaking occurring, but I have interviewed many witnesses who have. They simply say the being just dissolved in front of their eyes. The direct opposite is true, and these same witnesses would say they had also watched beings phase or pixelate into view, yes like in Star Trek or The Predator.

Wormy had explained the layout as the neighbor of the Adams' property, which by now we were calling Owl Moon. However, I did not explain all the neighbors. One of these neighbors is important to focus on and it was this neighbor I suspected may be capable of playing tricks on us. We called him Wormy due to his side hobby of collecting night-crawlers. He was an interesting neighbor for certain. He lived about 300 yards from Darrell on the next ridge over and had lived up there for over twenty years. Mostly, he was a lumberjack who sold lumber off his land to the local mill for profit, a common practice for those who own enough acreage to sell when money was slim. We would visit with Wormy periodically and bribe him with cheap beer to come by and tell us about the land and what he knew. I probed more than Darrell did and was trying to see just how much this local knew. The first thing of interest he told us was that he saw a weird drone in the woods one night. He said it was like a glowing white chandelier and would swing back in forth under the tree line. We asked him to tell us more, he said, "Not only did I see it that time, but one time it followed me to my house and waited for me when I hid around the corner." Very strange for a regular drone.

I asked him specifically about Sasquatch and he laughed while sticking his bowed arms out and itching his armpits like a gorilla cartoon. After initially laughing he said, "There was that blue-eyed bear." I said, "What man." Wormy insisted, "Ya, it was late one night in the winter when I went out to the woodshed to grab another log for the stove. As I walked up to the shed along the driveway, I see these glowing blue eyes staring at me from the road. I could see enough in the dark to know it was big and looking right in my direction." I looked back at Darrell who was listening, but I was unsure whether or not he was catching it all. I asked him to explain more. Wormy said, "Well it was just a blue-eyed bear, I guess, that approached me on two legs as I ran back into the house." I laughed and said, "You saw glowing blue eyes on something walking on two legs and you're still calling it a bear?" I could see I was going to get nowhere with Wormy and it was easier for him to call these things drones, chandeliers, and blue-eyed bears.

About two months after meeting Wormy a large red-skinned anomaly showed up on the front side of his forehead. It looked almost like a radiation burn. Nobody, including Wormy or the doctors, had a clue as to how it got there and what it was. As far as I know, he still has it and has no answers.

It did make Darrell and I wonder though. Once, while we were standing beside the outdoor deck, we saw something bright orange and red glowing behind Wormy's house. I broke out my FLIR camera to see if it was a fire in the chimney flue or him burning brush in the woods. The FlIR picked up nothing and as quickly as I grabbed the camera to film the light, it slowly winked out.

Wormy would also be gifted toys to his front porch. I believe he also gets small plastic dinosaurs and played it off as junk finding its way to him. He just wasn't curious about any of it, or he had his own thing going and did not want to share or admit it. Honestly, I think he knew way more than he let on, in fact, all the farmers around the area were holding back.

We decided not to stop with Wormy and so I pried harder in other places. I approached the single mom in the Yurt who lived in the abandoned apple orchard. I asked her if anything weird had happened to her while living up there and she said, "Maybe." I asked what she meant, and she explained there were three things. The first was she felt pinecones were being thrown at night against her Yurt walls. She said also that she thought someone was watching her through the windows. Windows that by no means were easily accessible up a long gravel driveway facing a dense tree line about 6 feet up. "Oh, and one more thing," she said, " my dad down the way lost his elderly cat. It just vanished and he assumed a coyote or cougar got him. Well, a couple of days after the cat went missing it turned up on his back deck in front of the sliding glass window with a flattened head. Nothing else was wrong with the cat as far as injuries." It seemed relevant to the activity and so I thanked her for her time. Soon after my visit she had a large sign posted on her private gravel drive saying NO TRESPASSING AND CAMERAS PATROLLING.

11

OILY SKIN

The shop where we kept the knees and Biggy was the first place Darrell found a handprint. It was shortly after the construction crew left when they completed the shop. Green metal ribbed siding housed the outer walls of the giant shop. Two Large metal remote-controlled garage doors faced the gravel driveway. I think it's safe to say you could have parked a small RV on both sides. The floor of the shop was a freshly-poured layer of smooth cement. There was only one regular hinged door that led out of the shop and followed onto the only cement walkway out front. That walkway would lead to the patio of the main house. The doors and door frames were painted with a bright fresh coat of primer. There was not a blemish on the shop, and it was a spectacular addition to the house and would increase the resale value. However, a couple of days after builders left Darrell noticed grayish oily handprints all over the top of the white doorframe. He called me over after work one day to look at it and we immediately took photos and videos of the scene. Just as a reminder, my cell phone was my main camera and video source like anyone else, although it barely got a reliable signal on Darrell's property. The fingers were wide, and the palm extended around the inside corner of the top ridge of the frame. In the middle of the door were two sets of fingerprints actually underneath the door jamb as though something tall was standing in the middle and had its hands and arms level with the top of the frame, which on average is 6.8 feet high. We zoomed in close with the camera and leaned in with our eyes. It was obvious to see skin folds or dermatoglyphics from where the hand was. We decided to lift the prints with what tools we had. I was even suggesting we remove the door, save it and replace it. In the end, we dusted and transferred the handprints via packaging tape. A quick note, this is not the best way to dust and transfer prints, a forensic kit with magnetic powder and fiber brush is strongly suggested. As a point, it is a lot of fun to play CSI, especially with suspected cryptids. The estimated measured size of the handprint we recovered was over 12 inches long. The average human male hand is only about 7.5 inches in length.

HUGE HAIRY HANDPRINTS

We asked the builders if perchance they may have had a big guy on the crew we never met who could have matched the handprints. He assured us that the crew we saw, was the crew that built it. We then sent him photos of the prints and said, "You gotta be kidding, look at the size, you guys." We had our answer as to rule out the builders and anyone else we knew. We honestly only had a few people over during most of this.

Another handprint collected was from Darrell's pickup truck. He came out to the front of his gravel drive and noticed the bungee cords usually strapped to the back of the open cab were now ripped off the plastic hooks and laying 5 feet away on the ground. I came home that afternoon to Darrell waiting for me with a roll of tape and transfer powders. I said where, and he pointed to the driver's side of the truck. Huge sausage-sized greasy fingertips on the dew saturated steel of Darrell's truck showed them perfectly. I grabbed my camera and filmed as Darrell pointed out one, two, three, four fingers. They slide up from the back cab of the driver's side pickup right where a broken hook from Darrell's bungee was left hanging. Whatever did this was in the cab when it tore it loose, or it was very tall with a huge arm length of 4-foot or more. If that was the case then it stood exposed with its back facing the front door of the house by the passenger side of the truck and reached over without its body touching the dew and dragged its finger up and snapped the cord. We again collected these huge fingertips and measured them. They were 1.5 inches wide at the tips whereas mine are only about 0.5 inches. They were also in perfect symmetry for something that drags its every spaced finger in a sliding motion around the smooth edges of an object.

One more greasy handprint was found in 2019 on the same shop door. This one was lower and flat up against the white door. It was again covered in a type of oil and even left behind a couple of hairs embedded in the oily fingerprint. These fingerprints have strange skinny bends to them. We collected the hair sample and copied the prints as we rolled the video. The size of the fingerprints looked average human-sized, that is until we dusted them and saw just how long they were.

12

PANOPTICON

We recorded constantly on the property. At one time, we would record using two recorders in the front and back of the property from 7 pm to 7 am for 4 months straight. Darrell and I would share the load downloading the audio onto our computers and inspecting the sounds via a visual sound analysis called a spectrogram, a process by way of visually analyzing the signature of sounds and inspecting these signatures as almost radar blips on the screen. The larger the sound, the larger the blip shows. It was through spectrogram we could take eight hours of audio and review it in only forty-five minutes. It helped speed up the process of constant recording and isolating what we thought was related. It was very obvious something was energetically happening on our audio with almost anywhere we put it. Initially, we would record what sounded like rocks being thrown and hitting the house, trailer, or shop. But we heard nothing land after it was hit. It didn't really matter where we stuck the recorders, you would always hear these energetic hits. There was never any lead-up to these sounds, like a bird flapping its wings or the sound of anything related to a physical act. In fact, most of these "hits" were very small to start with and then built up. Some nights it would be a chorus of rapid-fire hits or pops, other times it would just be plinking around off and on all night. Anything and everything sounds as if it was being hit by this phenomenon. You could hear wood, cement floors, plastic jugs, ladders, my boat, and trailer walls all being hit with something. We would hear what sounded like 2x4 boards slamming together and manmade objects quickly sliding around or being tossed. The shop was the epicenter for these sounds, but we didn't know it at first. We had to place our audio all around the front and back of the property to meet in the middle and see where it all came from. The shop, was it haunted? I was ready for certain surprises, but the shop always had the upper hand on how loud it would be. We of course ruled out heat expansion and cooling to metal siding. We ruled out critters and hoaxers. In fact, often the sounds would not happen when you were inside the shop, and the sounds would happen less when you were even near it. It was like the shop was aware or something inside of it was aware. On one occasion, around 6 am in the morning, Darrell and Cindy had gone off to work and I was out of town on business. Darrell had been recording in the shop the previous night and just left it running that morning. He got home and downloaded the audio like usual. He called me up and said, "We got a damn poltergeist again!" I came home to find the audio from that morning was recorded in the closed shop and taped the sound of what could only be a tornado throwing everything and anything at all areas of the shop. It was so loud, varied, and long that it was almost violent. Yet again, after going inside to inspect, nothing was moved or out of place. If it was a bird trapped, it would have to be the quickest bird on the planet, with no feathers and most likely dead in the corner. We decided to look at the area anywhere near the shop as a hotspot. It should be noted that loads of sounds were heard with gifts showing up near the southern wall of the shop. But we will get to that area soon enough.

The bedroom where we found the chalky white handprints was nearest to the shop. I asked Darrell more about that bedroom based on the unusual feeling I got when inside it. I am not sensitive, but that bedroom was strong enough vibe-wise, anyone could feel it. He said, "You know what's weird is yesterday I heard the kid that used to live here and stayed in that room … put a gun in his mouth." I asked, "He killed himself, yesterday?" Darrell said, "Ya, weird huh." I said to

Darrell, "When this family moved out of here and you bought it, did you get any info on where they were going and why they moved?" Darrell replied, "Well, all I know is they raised a bunch of kids here since they were babies and then suddenly sold it for a lot less than market value. I think they only live thirty minutes down the highway." My eyes were telling Darrell, this is important information we could have talked about long ago. He then said, "Oh, by the way, I've already been recording in Chucky's room and have not even reviewed it. I said, "Well let's do it."

It wasn't long before we found something very obvious on the recorder. Darrell had the recorder sitting on the windowsill facing inward with the window closed. We both agree we hear a young man's voice whispering, "I'm dead." Could it be related to the boy who killed himself? The boy was at least eighteen when he took his life, but the male voice sounded much younger.

Darrell would continue to record in that room for the next week and the pop and hit sounds were all we got. The weather was warming up, so he pointed the recorder out the window and directly at the shop. It was on that first night of opening the window that he recorded a single loud raspy laugh. To be honest, it sounded like a clip from Scooby-Doo. Just like you would hear in the cartoon. Talk about a contrast of two separate sounds. One made you think of purgatory and isolation, while the other was harmless and playful. This would be my introduction into the world away from just pops and hits and into the world of disembodied voices or EVPs. Was one related to the other? Was the boy who shot himself haunting his old room? Was Scooby-Doo one of his favorite cartoons? We had no idea, but the "Scooby laugh" can't be sound contamination on Darrell's end. It was recorded after they went to bed and the TV was never left on. Besides that, there were no other sounds except the laugh. It simply erupts and disappears.

CHUCKY'S ROOM KILLED SCOOBY

I contacted Sasquatch Researcher & sound analysis pioneer David Ellis. Ellis is widely respected in this small community and is a great resource for isolating and enhancing field audio. Perhaps Ellis could receive and send back enhanced clips of these sounds for us to review. I made the call and told him about the property from the beginning. I think he was excited about the possibilities and so were we. The initial sound files we sent off to Ellis were the two EVPs from the bedroom. It wasn't more than a couple of days when Ellis had shot me back an enhanced version of the two sounds and wrote at the bottom of the attached files, "What exactly am I listening to?" I was unsure what to say but I wanted to make sure I kept the conversations and assistance flowing, so I said, "weird I know."

I could tell him nothing of the weird stuff and be assured he would continue, or take a chance he probably ran into some weirdness like this before and just be curious enough to continue. Darrell and I called him, rather than email the strange details. I also had to make sure Darrell would vouch as a witness to this. The last thing I wanted was to be blamed for bad judgment or overhyping the explainable. Darrell and Ellis spoke for fifteen minutes and then I was handed back the phone. Ellis said we could send him any sounds we liked, but if we wanted to speed up the process I should learn to enhance sounds myself. It turned out to be something I was good at and found oddly addicting. So, I captured sounds as usual, but now with the addition of isolating them and enhancing the clarity.

Darrell reminded me he had an unused parabolic dish in his upstairs spare bedroom. The mobility and amplification of a parabolic gives you the flexibility to hear way out of the human range. It would stand to reason that you could hear for miles away if the conditions were right. Aside from the occasional log truck and dogs barking his backyard was the ideal spot to set it up. Darrell designed a crude but effective recording spot. All it took was a dining room chair and some packaging tape to strap it all together. I asked where he was thinking of aiming it, and he pointed to the wooded hillside behind his home. An important detail regarding these woods concerns the location of a familiar power line. The same stretch of power lines I had hiked through one evening and experienced the wall of jello. You could see them from the property, some 600-700 yards away. For most people that look long enough into Sasquatch sightings, they will note the significance of reports on or near stretches of power lines. What is interesting about that is the lack of other wildlife usually spotted feeding on these routes. That is to say, the power companies often spray weed-killing chemicals on the trails for needed access routes. Were we looking into the behavior of predator and prey, you would think it would be a perfect ambush spot for deer feeding in the open while a Sasquatch is waiting in the tree line. This does not seem to be the ideal spot for that, given the pesticides and EMF readings sparking down all over the perimeter.

After the 1st night of the parabolic sitting out in the backyard, Darrell awoke bright and early to preview the audio. I had gone to work for the evening and would be back later that morning to find him in the house looking for digital noise on the computer screen. He was scanning the audio and watching the waveform and taking clip after clip. I looked at his desktop monitor where he was dragging and dropping all these clips and said, "Is that all from just last night?" He said, "Ya man, you won't believe the sounds we've been missing." I asked him to play a clip through his factory desktop computer speakers. He hit play on the first sound and you could hear the normal hiss of ambient recording and the occasional frog ribbit. He smiled and looked at me as the audio suddenly went silent and then burst upon the waveform as a huge speaker cracking roar echoed from the mountains far away. It was just like you would imagine on any Sasquatch TV show opener. In fact, it almost sounded too good to be true, and I wanted to send it immediately to Ellis for review. Darrell said, "That's not all we got, there are major wood hit and pop sounds from all over the forest." The evening was filled with sounds far off, sounds we would have never caught with just our ears or laying out the recorders on windowsills. It became clear that the parabolic dish was a useful tool and would assist in helping to understand more about the phenomena.

13

UNLUCKY RABBIT

Something was almost always watching us and listening. We became more and more assured of that with every object or gift of significance left. As much as we were recording audio and video, something in return was keeping an eye and ear twice as much on us. Darrell's wife Cindy continued to get signs of this, although she seemed to think little of it. She asked for a bag of money and gold and in a crude but effective way, she gets a bag of berries and a golden brass rifle shell. Cindy is a strong woman, the kind that could survive and thrive when trouble comes her way. She was also no stranger to health issues. Not too long before she moved into the house, she had a major heart event that needs surgery. It wasn't too long after they moved in that Darrell finds a small glass heart appear below her hummingbird feeder. I at least find it a compelling and significant possibility something knew her health to some level and was leaving clues about that under something outdoors she cherished. I was always unsure how much of my enthusiasm towards these theories was benefiting the witness. Perhaps I should have led the witness less or not at all. Yet, the years prior to becoming friends with EESIs, I was fairly confident as to how the chessboard may progress. My job was to observe, respond and interpret quietly. I was becoming less disciplined at the last one.

While Biggy was in the closing stage of being built in late August 2018, I mentioned offhandedly that it would be amazing to get a hold of a taxidermy rabbit. I would place it by Biggy's feet near the terraformed platform he stood on. I talked to Eryn about online stores that might be a good place to order one and she suggested a few back. Perhaps even something more local would be a good fit, so the hunt was on.

I remember the Sunday very, very well. It was a hot day and directly after my live podcast Strange Bräu Radio downtown at Cottage Grove. The show went from 3-6 pm. After packing up my gear and heading back to Darrell's I parked my car and looked out over the trailer for more gifts. I hopped out and began my routine of looking atop the trailer roof and everywhere else. Then I saw it. A fresh kill was laid out and set in front of my trailer. It was a freshly dead Cotton Tail Rabbit sprawled out lengthwise on its side. I walked up and immediately recorded the video. It was so fresh there was barely any glaze to its dead eyes or any bugs, which was weird in this heat. I ran out to the main house and knocked on the backdoor. I picked up my phone as usual and began recording. Darrell followed me as I led him to the sight. His first words were, " Oh my gosh, that was not there earlier." He then assures me he didn't kill it. I roll video as I lean in with a small stick and examine it. We flip it over a couple of times and see no bite marks or broken bones. If it was predation that took it out, it did so untraditionally. As I examine, Darrell comments on the recent large footprint he saw in the driveway, which ordinarily would have been a big deal. I focus on the rabbit and flip it over onto its other side. There's blood drying on the fur and down deep to the skull. I pick at the injury and notice a rock buried in the bone. The rock was small but bigger than a bullet. It's possible the rock somehow embedded itself from the gravel driveway into the skull if the animal was dropped from the sky, perhaps by a bird? But given everything else that had happened, I leaned into Darrell with my camera and asked him what he thought. He said, "I think they killed it because you and I were talking about it." I was completely freaked out and thrilled all at once. What if! The rabbit was so fresh it looked like a delivery right before I pulled up in the drive. We lifted up the rabbit and considered doing a full direction or necropsy, but that was stirring away from the new possible and likely gift of significance. I immediately call Eryn in Washington and relate the story to her. I show her the video, the photos, and tell her about the blow by blow. I hear a new silence over the phone...worry. I assure her I'm fine but don't know what my next move should be. She suggested I immediately get rid of it and not push my luck; something is listening, and it's granting wishes...and now something had died.

DEAD BUNNY

I take a breath and struggle with what appears to be obvious interaction. I try relating to her over the phone the similarities of something akin to a tribe of Indians meeting explorers. Perhaps they were wanting to trade. Again, I hear Eryn say, "Back down and get rid of it! You need to set boundaries and this is way over the line," I hesitantly agreed, if not only to squelch her worry. I grabbed the rabbit and took it down to the creek. I again talk to the tress as I stand with the kill in hand. "Whoever you are, I think I know, but you cannot kill for me! I mean, yes...WE DO kill for us...and that's how I would have gotten the rabbit eventually, but that's NOT YOUR job!" I heard myself say all this and hear what you may hear to conflict. I bend down with the now stiff dead rabbit. I grabbed its ankle and twisted until I heard a snap. I twisted the rabbit foot until it popped in my hand and broke loose. I then swung the rabbit out over the creek current and watched it sink down out of view. I walked back with the rabbit foot in hand and wondered if I had made a critical error. Was I overreacting? I did what I could at the moment to make a decisive reaction, but honestly, I don't know what the right move was.

I called Eryn and told her not to worry as I privately held the severed foot in my hand. I could hear the obvious concern in her voice but was still conflicted as to if I made the right move. It was, after all, something I was looking for, only fresher and more direct. But what if I said something more extreme about something I wanted dead, like, "I hate that SOB, and I wish they were dead." It was these thoughts that Eryn reminded me of, and I agreed. I really had no idea what killed it, although Sasquatch was at the top of my list. I looked down at the severed foot in my hand and knew that if I kept it, I was permitting the offering. The thought was enough to make me go back to the creek and throw the remainder of the rabbit back over the edge.

After that moment there was a conflict between Eryn and me regarding what we were calling the Owl Moon Lab. It was a very specific moment that seemed tied to what we privately talked about. You have to understand I'm an adrenaline junkie and I'm willing to incite activity now and accept the consequences later. When you have loved ones around you with your best interests at heart, they want to protect you from those consequences. I felt like their protection would hinder studying the possibilities. I came to terms with the kill and wanted to move on to a new chapter, but there was unfinished business still. Before Eryn hung up the phone that day she said something that caught more than my ear. She said, "Well on the bright side thank God they didn't bring ya a snake, you hate those."

Three days later around the same time of day in the exact same spot to the inch where the dead rabbit was laid out, I find a freshly decapitated snake. It was so fresh when I found it the meat bees had only recently discovered it. The head laid only a few inches away, untouched and un-mangled. I rolled the video once again and call for Darrell. He assures me he didn't kill it and it wasn't there earlier. This was either a prank or a bad joke. I looked at the gruesome scene and scan the woods all around waiting to hear something laughing at my expense.

I call Eryn and she is in shock with the rest of us. I show her the video and say, "I'm keeping it, I hate it, but I have to." It was a throw down to the rabbit and a show of force that yes, it was us, and yes, we hear you and we have a twisted sense of humor. I couldn't be scared off by it and, as much as I hate snakes, I decided the only thing to do was preserve it. We let it decompose, which happened in less than twenty-four hours after the bugs and heat decomposed it. I slide the remains in an Altoid can and taped it shut. I grabbed a marker and wrote in big bold letters "THE FEAR CAN." I still have it stored away with so many of the other gifts. Periodically, when I'm facing a fear head-on, I will mentally picture the can and face the fear.

BEHEADED SNAKE

After this moment we were on a different footing with our unseen neighbors. It would be the only time we would have something likely killed on our behalf. It took me back to 2011 at Earl's place when I found that dead rodent pinched in half with blood freshly oozing from it. In a similar fashion, neither of these kills had signs of being attacked by an animal. The snake and rodent looked to be recently pinched or torn in half.

Laying out fresh kills or bits and pieces of dead animals is something very common for ESSIs. They're usually placed somewhere you can see them or directly in front on a path. Yes, it's a bit Godfather-esque, i.e.-*the horse head in the bed.* But I have to wonder if there's a deeper cultural divide by The Tailor than just mere gruesome trickery.

14

THE HEBRONS

C ottage Grove, Oregon, was settled in the year 1848 and for the most part, it was a western town like any other. A virgin valley filled with salmon and trout in every river and lake, and tall old grown Fir and Cedar trees perfect for building with. Aside from this, there was *gold in them there hills*. It was known for a mining district called Bohemia, which for its time was a city. Hidden atop the steep mountain peaks, 5500 ft in elevation, where the quartz and gold merged. Bohemia City would even house a general store, post office, and reportedly a brothel. The town of Cottage Grove was over forty miles away from Bohemia and it would take a horse and wagon days to travel to and from for supplies.

Between these two cities is what is now known as Cottage Grove Lake, but at the time was a valley floor where pioneers had settled, and most likely near tribes of Kalapuya Indians. It was in this valley the Hebron Church was built. A sect of fundamentalist Christians that wanted a place to freely worship. Their influence was enough in the community that you can still find street names associated with the town and perhaps a few people that were related to Hebron.

Darrell and I discovered this group and went down to the lakebed when it was dried up. Reportedly on the South end of the lake, you could find the old foundation to the small church that was built down there. We ended up finding it quickly and could see where the fireplace was and the small foundation square around it. We even found a couple of iron forged nails still laying in the mud. Darn impressive given the years and the fact the lake is filled up and drained every year. We took the finds home and never thought any more about it.

I started to privately wonder if the Hebrons were linked to the land. Perhaps there was a few ghostly holdouts that were messing around on or near where Darrell and Cindy lived. Or was it something the Hebrons awoke and never sent back? It was a worthwhile angle to pursue, and I had time to look into it.

I think it's important to mention religion and spirituality. My upbringing was convenient Christianity. What I mean by that is my family was largely all Protestant and attended regular church functions, but it did not affect our immediate cultural perspective. I was raised to believe the Bible was superior to all books but was never made to read it. I was asked to attend a non-denominational church sometimes, but my family was rarely satisfied with the sermon or pastor. It was their opinion the old ways were better and that Prosperity Preaching or Charismatic Christianity was secularism infiltrating truth. I even taught a home ministry for a while, inviting people into our house weekly for digging deeper into the nature of God.

Those years left me feeling like a fraud. I mostly had to pretend to be their version of Christian so I could get along with the whole. It wasn't as though I was a total sham, I did find there was evidence of miracles in the scriptures, but I always wanted to dig deeper into the how and why. I couldn't take the written word and run with it, and I never felt the personage of Christ entering my heart and being reborn. I may have said I did to make my folks satisfied, but I was never honest with them or myself. I write this because it's hard and honest and most Christians, maybe even the Hebrons, want the assurance of Salvation after they die. They never invest in what the scriptures are filled with, the supernatural. Instead, the Christians doubt the supernatural or chastise it as evil. The only time the supernatural is appreciated is when recognized as obviously angelic. The day I saw those lights in Oz were as close to angelic as you could get without actually seeing halos and trumpets. However, when I told the story to my family, they were unimpressed and suspect as to what demonic source was at play. It should have transformed them and moved their faith closer to God, instead, I was looked at as a dupe for being tricked by the Devil's snares.

I don't entirely throw that notion out. I do think it's good and evil and a war on for men's freedom of will. Is the Devil the soul co-conspirator for this mission, I don't think so. It's a sticky question I like to leave up to scholars who plunge into the apologetic in a more thought-provoking way. If I were to suggest who supports this, I would suggest CS Lewis's book The Screwtape Letters. The story is written from a demon's perspective and is a tutorial on how demons teach other demons clever ways to steer man away from God. If we were being *Screwtaped* at the Owl Moon Lab, I think there would have been some darkness that arose in our presence. We just were never getting the vibe of evil. It was like nature was showing its true colors and all its impossibilities.

Synchronicities regarding the name Hebron presented itself firstly with an Amazon order Darrell made. In searching for a better way to study or interact with the phenomena, Darrell wanted to have eyes and ears on the property twenty-four seven. He ended up purchasing a high-end baby monitor with remote video, a moving camera lens, and a two-way radio. It arrived not long after he made the order. He called me into the main house and said, "Holy crap, man, this thing is made in Hebron, Israel." What we're the chances of that, I would say slim to none.

Then there was the Hebron glassware incident where Eryn is suddenly gifted a single wine glass by a mutual friend. The glass is unique and shaped like any other wine glass, however, it's fire glazed in the most beautiful aquamarine. These glasses are prized possessions for collectors and fetch a pretty penny. I had never even heard of Hebron, let alone their imports like baby monitors and wine glasses.

HEBRON GLASS

I looked up the name and its history. It turns out Hebron is an ancient settlement that dates to Biblical antiquity. Well, to be fair, most cities all reach back to post Genesis timelines. Hebron sits upon the West Bank, on the Palestinian border of Israel. The interesting scriptural note about the city of Hebron is written about in the Book of Judges. It speaks of a time where many years later, after the forty years of wandering had come to an end, and the younger generation of Israelites had the faith to cross over the Jordan River, and take the land of Canaan from the Anakim and other giants who dwelt there, when it came time to divide the land of Canaan amongst the tribes of Israel, it is discovered that Caleb was given the city of Arba, which belonged to Arba, who was the father of Anak the giant.

> "And they gave Hebron unto Caleb, as Moses said: and
> he expelled thence the three sons of Anak."
>
> — *Judges 1:20, KJV*

> "And unto Caleb the son of Jephunneh he gave a part
> among the children of Judah, according to the

commandment of the LORD to Joshua, even the city
of Arba the father of Anak, which city is Hebron. And
Caleb drove thence the three sons of Anak, Sheshai,
and Ahiman, and Talmai, the children of Anak."

— *JOSHUA 15:13-14, KJV*

It was hard to ignore the link between the city of Hebron and the story
of giants, Anakim and Nephilim. This being the Biblical account of
fallen angels who were cast out from Heaven along with
Lucifer/Satan/Saturn *the light barrier.* The Nephilim took the
daughters of men and raped them, making offspring of hybrids,
essentially a race of demigods that have an attribute of humans and
spirit beings. The Nephilim are spoken of not only in biblical circles
but ancient alien theorists and cryptozoologists. They theorize the
bloodline of the Nephilim that explains the supernatural and spiritual
nature of the phenomena. Whatever the truth was regarding Hebron
and Giants, it seemed a familiar odd coincidence we were in Sasquatch
hotspot, and down the street, the old Hebron settlement was built.
What if the westward pioneers that settled here, who were all mostly
Christians, witnessed Sasquatch and named the land like in the Book
of Joshua. It seems plausible to expect them to do so. However, why
would they settle here at all if it was filled with what they would
perceive as evil?

15

LIVING GLOW

I previously wrote about a hillside I called Oz. This would be my introduction to orbs or living lights. The lights or orbs are alive. That is my consensus. Seeing them three times now before the Owl Moon Lab, I feel as though what is being described as orbs or balls of light are alive. They have an organic living light quality to them that is probably best demonstrated with a creature that emits bioluminescence. These lights float and emit from the air in various shapes and sizes, but most of the traditional orbs are not a huge burst of white energy but small white baseball-sized energy forms. They can float any matter of direction and fade out as quickly as they fade in. They can flash open and closed in a second or slowly sink into the forest canopy.

I mentioned that I saw them in Oz, but I had seen them one other time above the spot where my son had his brief sighting. On that night they appeared above our parked cars as the sunset and were not only white but green, red, and orange. The group with me photographed them as they came over us and flicked off and on. I recall standing there watching the event and then hearing something flick over the brim of my baseball hat. It sounded like a zippo lighter being rubbed to ignite, I thought it was that. I looked around and saw the group was all standing with their hands in their pockets. That is when I heard another sound, this time it sounded like a rock being tossed at the truck. I looked deep in the woods with my flashlight but saw nothing. The lights eventually all phased out of view one by one, and we left.

The Lab had its own share of lights. Wormy, the farmer on the neighboring hill, described what he called the drone or the chandelier, a fascinating description of lights following him and swinging through the trees. Darrell saw this light on several occasions while standing in his backyard. He even filmed it and said it moved like a laser on the wall, quick unpredictable movements or something that could change circumference like the iris of a pupil. He said on more than one occasion that he saw it swing at low altitudes over his house without making a sound and burped out a little ufo below it. "They kind of fell out of it like pollen off a flower," he said. He even filmed some amazing footage of it one night that showcased its sporadic flight pattern and dilating core.

Once, while standing out on his deck in the full sunlight of a spring afternoon, Darrell would record what looked like a gliding propane tank. It looked to have no contrail, missing tail and wings, no signature marks or insignia, no sound and almost gliding more than flying. It was solid white and tube-looking, much like a pill or tank, or perhaps even a tic-tac.

SKY PHENOMENA

Another night Darrell and Cindy said they were asleep upstairs and their whole bedroom filled with white light. It was described as pure white and had no particular source other than the light outside. They couldn't pinpoint any more than that and said as quick as it was there that it winked out.

I saw my first light at The Lab on one of the night walks towards the creek. It was as we were making our way back from the sheepdog's farm and walking into a darkened area of the path. We rarely used flashlights and used the terrain and sky to navigate our way. As we approached the creek, the same one I disposed of the rabbit, we both saw a basketball-sized white orb float down the hill and phase-out of view when it hit the road. It was fluid like it was underwater but floating in the sky. Darrell had never seen one like that before and it was the biggest and most stable sighting of an orb I had ever seen. The whole sighting lasted about three seconds or less.

Darrell would see orbs like that again in that approximate location ten months after our sighting and describe them as precursors to Sasquatch activity. Heavy circular footfall all around them, a deathly shit smell filling the air, and electronic malfunctions.

The night walks were great ways of seeing possible UFOs on clear nights. One evening we left the house on our regular trajectory to the creek and about 100 yards away from the property we see large white and red objects silently roam parallel with us at low orbit. It moved silently above us with no marker lights and was not the orbit of the ISS. Darrell grabbed his camera and recorded video and just as he aimed the lens at the UFO, it flashed a bright light and his camera phone died. The battery wasn't dead, but the system malfunctioned enough that he couldn't use it at the moment he needed it. The UFO faded upwards and was never seen again.

We thought well maybe we can put up a motion sensor game that came out the front of the house and just see for ourselves what will mess with it. I could tell Darrell was curious, but I had my doubts it would help. I thought for sure we would never catch more than blurs and deer. I was wrong. The first weird image he caught was of what happened to be a free-floating bar of light that appears on three shots taken as it floated into view. Above this bar of light was a box of light.

They moved as a unit on the three photos and were about 4 feet off the ground and about 24 inches in length. We tried to rule out them being a double shot exposure, somehow of a pickup truck's headlights, but we could not. It's important that these bars or boxes of light have been seen moving horizontally in the woods where Sasquatch is present.

The next strange photo came from the same game cam. It showed the only lens of the camera was being obstructed, that it was being covered for over thirty frames. The lens showed a blurry striation of light and dark lines curving down from the top-right frame to the bottom left of the frame. They almost looked like hairs pushed up against the lens, maybe fur. The other interesting aspect of it was the camera had a temp gauge and the temperature went up 7 degrees as the subject leans up against the camera. It could have been hair from Raccoon, rodent, or even cat but it was not a deer. Darrell had that camera up high in the tree so it made no sense for it to be deer.

GAME CAM ANOMOLIES

16

SHOPTALK

By the middle to late summer of 2018, our audio recording skills had gotten good. I had learned there was an even better and more effective way to recover more hidden sounds on my spectrogram. I could turn over a 12-hour recording session in about an hour and a half with at least 3-5 good quality anomalous sounds. The sounds again ranged from small to big hits and knocks to other more ghostly or cryptic sounds. Unlike the little boy's voice that whispered clearly, "I'm Dead" these vocals were difficult to decipher. We also found that most of these language or voice sounds had a specific place, a sweet spot. For the most part, the shop was that spot, and a specific spot on the wall of the shop. We wondered why there of all places, and what was in the shop that could attract the phenomena? As we scanned inside and out looking for clues such as old relics or markers, I looked at Biggy. He was nearly complete and towered over us at 8.5 feet tall. Could it be him? Was something attracted to the model I had made? Did they see it as a type of idol I had built in honor of them? We stood in the shop and talked about the timeline between the first sign of activity and Biggy. It was too soon for that to be the answer, but maybe time didn't matter to Sasquatch...if that was what all this was. The one thing that did match the timeline was the knee impressions.

They were housed in the same shop and stuck right next to Biggy. Could it be the impressions were an attractant? There are stories from those that say Sasquatch hair has its own power and is something you should never take home with you. We had gobs of suspected Sasquatch hair collected and some of these hairs were literally poking out of the plaster cast.

BIGGY

We had so many guesses as to how and why, and any theory was better than nothing. So we recorded a lot and came back with a lot.

Nine times out of ten, we would get good audio. If we did not get EVPs, we got tremendous hits, pops, and slaps. Sometimes we would get the hits, pops, or slaps with an EVP. You would hear pop, hit or slap right before, during, or after the vocal. The recorder was the only thing in the shop, for the most part, unless Darrell had set up the baby monitor. However, the Hebron baby monitor didn't show up until 2019.

The voices were rarely heard by our own ears, at least the ones in the shop or near the shop. The only exception to that would be the large vocals from the wilderness, usually after 10 pm.

Types of sounds

- Tesla Coil buzz sound.
- The sound of stone rolling or sliding on stone. We would catch that outside, but it sounded more pronounced inside the shop. This sound was creepy and reminded me of a granite slab sliding open in a shallow tomb, like in an old horror movie.
- Things landing on the cement floor and breathing or panting loudly near the recorder and then slowly fading off.
- Large sonic wave-type bangs or gunshot sounds. You could hear what sounded like the air getting sucked out of the room and gathering energy before it exploded. Once, while sleeping outside near the back of the shop, I heard this sound myself. It was so loud that I covered my ears and fell backward out of my chair. The sound was less than 10 feet away.
- EVP | ghostly child voice that screams either "Toby, get back" or "hold me, get back."
- EVP | layered chaotic screams of multiple voices yelling something simultaneously. During this clip you can hear a split second of English as someone yells with reverberation, "Now can there be any other reason."
- EVP | murmuring or whispering.
- EVP | An old man inside the shop or just outside the shop saying something like "you home?"
- EVP | Someone breathing or sighing next to mic head.
- Sound of three knocks on the cement, like knuckles hitting the floor.
- Someone blowing three times, like someone trying to blow out candles.
- Magnets we set up in the shop colliding together. You would hear them distinctively slam together on audio review, and yet they would be separated when you found them.

EVPS AND OTHER STRANGE SOUNDS

There would be nothing disturbed in the garage after these sounds, no matter how chaotic the audio clip. The one exception to that was one evening when Darrell walked into the shop to grab something he needed. As he opened the door, he felt a strange sensation sweep over his skin and there spinning on the floor was an empty pop can. He still talks about that being the scariest moment he had. He got off easy.

Our recorders were never hidden, in fact, the only time they were not out in the open is when they were out the shop and sitting in the open air. There was a lot of unpredictable weather, as is usual for the PNW. Mic heads, digital buttons, and batteries don't like cold moist air, so in those times we would either not record or stick the recorder in a spot not exposed to the elements. Our intent was never to camouflage, but to protect the tech. We hardly ever had battery drain issues, which is odd for a property that was as active as The Lab. If we did have issues with our electronics, it was almost always on Darrell's end, and usually directed to his cell phone. It was not uncommon for Darrell to get his phone suddenly turned off or for him to have sudden interference. On at least two occasions his phone would suddenly be taken over or power off. On one occasion, while we were doing our usual night walks on the logging roads nearby his home, we saw a strange light in the sky. It was traveling a usual commuter jet flight path parallel to our walk on the road. It was a bright white light that could have been mistaken for a satellite. It hovered at a low orbit, we assumed, and then powered up and became even brighter as it slowly moved away. Darrell grabbed his smartphone and pointed it at the light above. As he aimed his phone at the light it burst a giant white flash all around its core. Darrell watching this on his screen said, "WOW," followed by, "Oh Crap." I looked over to Darrell as he mentioned, "my phone just turned off. I know it's charged." We then watch the light simply drift into a smaller pinprick. It almost appeared to aim away and elevate its position to a higher orbit or altitude. Darrell would not be able to operate his phone for the remainder of the walk.

17

CONSTANT VISITORS

By the fall and winter of 2018/19, we had realized that yes, there were particular areas where the activity spiked, but it was anywhere and everywhere. The shop was just a piece of it, and we can only guess why. We found that just outside the shop there was also a sweet spot as I mentioned before by the metal wall. It was here I would set up my lawn chair for the evening and wait to hear and perhaps see something inexplicable, maybe a Sasquatch...maybe better.

The Sasquatch-type vocals we caught were largely ignored by people I thought would be more interested. I knew what we had as far as vocals because I'd heard all that was available. We were in a different category of proof than most. We had nothing to do with the weighty evidence that came our way, we just stood with a wide fishing net. The audio we collected is a piece of evidence that, for starters, shows consistency of probable Sasquatch language.

I would mail these sounds off to David Ellis and he, in return, would send an immediate response and get to work. Each suspected Sasquatch vocal would generally have some physical evidence left behind to tell a story. We tried not to tie too many loose threads, but it all fell into place, especially when DNA possibilities started being handed to us.

Types of Suspected Sasquatch Sounds

- High pitch screams from nearby and far off. These sounds were preceded or buried under the sounds of all the dogs in the valley barking and howling. Coyotes as well, but usually just house dog sounds.
- Moans that turned into a siren yell. The classic sound you may hear on a typically Sasquatch show.
- Tongue click or mouth pop sounds at close range.
- Wood knock sounds from far off.
- Trees being ripped down or out of the ground.
- Large footprints stomping, running or tiptoeing.
- Grunts & growls.
- Talking with percussive huffs. These sounds impressed us because you could tell the individual was far off and when they percussively huff, the sound travels like a sonic wave right to the microphone. You can feel it as much as hear it.
- Speech of an unknown language. Something modulated its voice from high to low in seconds.
- EVP | ghostly Sasquatch moan.

SASQUATCH VOCALS

Scientist, EESI, and Author Henry Franzoni was invited over for pizza one night and sat with us near the newly built fire pit just outside the shop. He listened to our experiences and talked about the work of Nikola Tesla. He explained that so much of the unseen world is untapped energy and we had to discover how to tap into it. He suggested that the shop may be a giant Tesla coil of sorts, like a supernatural beacon sitting atop an environmentally charged area. The term Geomanced was used in further describing how this could be done by either ceremony over a sacred spot or that it was always here and just accessed by the Sasquatch and the others. The fire glow slowly dimmed as, one by one, the guests all left for bed and pretty soon it was just Henry, me and Darrell. Then Henry took a sharp right turn into music and drumming. He said, "I'm a drummer, professional drummer, I guess some would say...I know a bit about music and how good drumming affects it." We listened intently to Henry's cool way of laying out an even more interesting theory. Henry went on, "It is not only the sound of drumming the spirit uses to access this world, but it is the beats between them." I asked what he meant? He said, "Well all I know is there is something to it, the vibration between the beats is what they dig...and there's something to do with a 6-beat rhythm and in particular three 6-beat rhythms." 666? I thought to myself, gulp...what have I got myself into? It wasn't long before that final comment Henry got into his car and drove away. If there was ever an untapped resource of Sasquatch knowledge it would be Henry and his brain.

Only a couple days after Henry left we kept recording all over the property, including the shop. The sweet spot in the shop was inside pointing out towards an old un-installed outlet box. I would simply stick my recorder in there and face it to the outside area where the gravel drive was connected to metal walls. It was just outside the shop on the ground where a lot of gifts were set and glyphs made. It was in this spot we recorded something again happening all at once with no approach in the lengthy gravel drive. It would have taken a Ninja or Tom Cruise in Mission Impossible lowering himself on a cable to pull this move. Unless it was just straight out of Star Trek.

We hear drums, in particular the sounds of something drumming on the empty 50-gallon metal barrel sitting at the outer edge of the shop. It is close, less than 10 feet away as the rhythmic beats are softly padded down. Not like a hard object striking steel, but bongo hand hits. Soft and deliberate syncopations. We don't know what the technical term is for the rhythm or if there's a way to measure what beat it is. Then, the vocals start. The drumming stops and then close to the shop wall are snarling percussive moans and gasps. It reminded me of monkeys fighting in the wild, perhaps over territory or an item. You can hear it slowly fade away from the shop wall and into the distance. Just fading monkeys from the barrel. This was a joke never planned, to literally be talking about a barrel of monkeys floating off into the ether.

FRANZONI DRUM ROLL

I called Franzoni the next day and sent him the sound file. I said, "Henry I think they know you and heard your theory on drumming." He laughed and said, "I know that man." That was it from Henry. That was it for that amazing audio. It never happened before that day or since. Henry did reach out again via email and suggested we look more into the layers of our recordings. He theorized it was between the layers of audio and video recording that the supernatural will present itself. The more layers you lay out, the more likely you will find an EVP or interaction. So we came up with a plan on how to increase our recordings.

The plan was to always record video while recording audio if time permitted and to record audio with as many recorders as possible. It was our hope that the layers between video and audio would help us solve the riddle, or at least have us asking better questions. We would also use the shop as an isolation booth for Guiana pigs willing to participate. Hell, we were the Guinea pigs as well and wanted to get confirmation it was not just us. So we would take the recorder in the shop and leave it near one of us or a willing participant. We would feed a 50-foot-long cord from the headset jack on the recorder and into a speaker. Then we would turn out the lights or wait till dark and close the door behind them. Then we would wait by the speaker and listen to what happened. Plenty did.

We sent twelve people into that shop with the door closed and listened. On certain occasions they would hear someone walking in the gravel outside the shop when nobody was there. We would not hear the sound on the speaker, but they would. On another occasion we sent someone in there who heard along with us a huge, massive crash inside and then a percussive swinging and rhythmic clanking. Then there were the moans captured on video as we recorded the speaker with my camera. These ghostly moans are super loud on video and coming from inside the shop...but we could not hear them with our own ears.

EVP MOAN

In the Fall of 2018, I was getting ready to finish Biggy and set him up for my radio show at the neighborhood pub. Darrell and I slowed down our research during a job change and my needing to move closer to work. I asked Darrell if he would be up for having one final sleep out on the property. He agreed and talked about what we should have set up for the evening. He blew up his king-size air mattress and I set up my rigid cot. We opened both sets of large shop and side doors where the fingerprints had been found. I set my recorder down between us on the cement deck and plugged in my headphones. I talked to Darrell periodically as 10 pm rolled around. I could tell neither of us would last all night and someone would either go inside to the comfort of their own bed or pass out in the cold. It turned out we both passed out around 11:30 pm.

Around 12:45 I awake to my phone alarm going off, signaling it was time to check my recorder and make sure my old rechargeable batteries are not dead. I struggle to grab my cell phone to shut off the loud ringtone and secure it. I yawn and scrape around on the cold cement floor for my recorder. As I lean over to reach for it on my left, I see something coiled around the base. I grab my headlamp and click it on. I see it is a large piece of cord splayed out. I lean up out of my seat and squirm out of my mummy bag to observe it better. I wake Darrell immediately, "Dude, Darrell, did you leave a piece of rope or cord on the ground next to me?" He snored back, "What?" I said, "DARREL, wake up! Did you leave this cord next to me last night?" Again, a groggy Darrell squints in my headlamp glare, "No man what?" He leans out and over the side of his air mattress. As he gets his baring I study the cord more. It looked to be a 3-foot long strand of green paracord woven to another piece of cord, like a braid. In fact, it was braided from the middle of the cord so it was looped in over itself. The green bit was the outer shell of the nylon sheath that makes paracord so strong. The inside sheaths were smaller white cords within this nylon tube for added strength. The most common use for the cord is parachuting or camping.

I turned on all the shop lights and insisted on Darrell looking at it to make double sure he did not drop it out of his air mattress on a previous camping trip. He assured me no way and thought it very strange. He asked me where I found it laying and I said, "Right between us on my recorder, a couple feet from me." I considered taking a listen to the recorder, but it would require a certain amount of setting up and disturbing the quiet landscape, so I simply put the cord back down next to me, as well as the recorder, and said thank you. I then walked out to the large gravel driveway and sat for an hour in a lawn chair. At one point, I heard in the apple orchard a woman's voice. But, there was that single mom in the Yurt way back there, maybe she got up and said something outside. I asked for whatever was leaving us gifts to please keep doing so and could they reach out and touch me. I waited with my arms splayed open and a camera inside pointing at me. The cold air rolled down from the mountains and into the valley as I waited, listened and spoke. After about forty-five minutes I got up from the chair and got back into my mummy bag on the cot. I laid flat on my back and tried to listen without sleeping. I think Darrell went back to sleep fairly quickly, long before this moment. I did not ask so I assume his snoring was legit and not manufactured. I ended up falling back to sleep while the camera and recorder rolled in front and out towards the trees and drive.

At 4:55 am I felt something that woke me. My eyes quickly popped open as I felt my body push to the left. I thought for sure I was moving in my sleep, perhaps on a thin elevated cot I was about to roll off, so I repositioned myself and laid there awake looking at the recorder, now dead again. A moment later I felt myself moving to the left of the cot by the paracord and recorder, only this time I was awake and appreciated what was taking place. Whatever was occurring was not me moving on my own. The way I always describe it is the best way I know how; It was like being caught between the reverse ends of a magnet's polarity. There's no gravity pulling them together but pushing them apart. I felt the sensation surround my whole body and slide me to the left and then set me down, maybe only an inch or less but enough for me to appreciate the whole experience. I gasped for Darrell, but he slept on. There was nothing scary about it but oddly it felt natural somehow. I asked aloud and whispered to the air, "Do it again." After a minute it happened a third time. I was being levitated and I was awake. I could hear the fabric from the mummy bag slide under me as it barely passed the nylon of the cot. I never toyed with the idea it was an OBE, out-of-body experience, how could I when I was awake. And as far as I'd heard, nobody ever slid like a game of air hockey before their spirit left their body. After the third "session" I woke up from my bag and walked back out to the gravel drive. I asked, "Did you want to get me up, do you want me to see something or meet you?" I looked up into the clear night sky and saw Orion's belt hover above the Doug Firs. I did not go back to sleep and instead grabbed my recorder and set up my laptop. I couldn't wait till morning and was obviously being interacted with by some invisible force. I thought to myself, "I just fucking levitated, wait did I technically fly?" I mean it was a brief flight, but I guess it counts. I did ask for them to touch me at 1 am, maybe this was part of that? My mind raced at what was happening and I could not upload the night quick enough.

I time stamp everything before I record it so I can quickly get in and out of a session without guessing. This night was no different. I turned on my laptop and zoomed in on the spectrogram data, and then I saw something. Around 12:40 pm I follow the rhythm of Darrell's snore and see a small blip on the lower Hz of the screen. I listen and hear something slide and possibly land or abruptly stop, but there was nothing walking and certainly nothing approaching. Then I hear them, a statement from the mystery woman.

The first sound is from an individual saying something loud and distinctly feminine.

It just burst onto the recorder with no lead-up and sounds, like it's less than 10 feet from us as we slept. As she's speaking there's a giant hit, slap or knock on the third word or sound. Then there's the sound of a lounge click or maybe someone snapping their fingers, a click of some kind.

The second sound is another female voice that speaks very robotically and rehearsed. Her statement is just about as long as the first but is spoken with a different tone. The first was singsongy but the second was kind of programmed.

The third sound follows right after the second and is also female but distant. It sounds far away and down a hall. Only thing is, there are no halls in the shop so it's another mystery. It's a fast-spoken phrase that just sounded unrelated to the first and second.

The fourth sound was directly after the third and also female. Her voice reminds me of the first sound and is very conversational and almost sweet. There was a nurturing quality to her tone and phrasing.

The fifth sound is immediately after the fourth and stops. You can hear a small quiet phrase for about a half-second. It sounded again like a female, and I think she was asking a question.

Here is what we heard phonetically and a time count for each phrase 1-5:

1. *DISS-SIS-YADGE-MOTCHKAH* 3 sec. | Female A
2. *YETZUS-QUPER-WE-BESAH-YU* 3 sec. |Female B
3. —UNTRANSLATED—1.5 sec. | Female C
4. *MEE-DJAH…YU-MASH-GOOT-DAH-HODAP…GOOTOO-GO-YABUTT* 4 sec.|Female A
5. *DUN-WINAH* 1 sec. | Female C

The language part was obvious, but how and who? I could tell immediately that whoever was on that recorder seemed close and not far. However, did that mean they were purely physical and in the same area as us, or did it mean they were perhaps nonphysical and only transmitted well. There was so much to go over, but first I had to take a minute to appreciate the catch. I doubted there would be any natural explanation for the sounds and here is why.

The voices and phrases SOUND LIKE THEY ARE between AT LEAST TWO females who correspond before and after statements in a very natural way. They each speak loudly and with authority. Within the first statement, there's a huge pop or hit. This was a classic sign for us that an EVP or paranormal sound was responsible. Also, there is this broadcast quality to the whole 15-second moment. It reminded me of an old tube radio from the 30s, finding a frequency and adjusting just for them to squeeze out the conversation and then fade away. However, we possessed no such radio, only our phones and a recorder. There was no way for it to be blamed on the farm next door or Darrell's house. It was just too close and clear. I woke Darrell around 6 am and shared everything. He couldn't believe it and nor could I. The following is an email between Dave Ellis and his anonymous contact on the East Coast. This person I once spoke with on the phone and he assured me he's qualified to determine the language, and that it was a language. The only reason he does not go by his given name is due to job security. The code name he goes by is Mononga Hela. This is our last response about the audio of the mystery woman.

WOW! That's a pretty amazing audio capture. Those voices couldn't be too far away from his position.

No, they were befuddled, as was I about how close the voices were. Brazen isn't even the word. People would be concerned with waking them up talking that loudly. Makes no sense.

I'm not sure I hear anything special when I slow it down, but I do make these observations after a few passes. I am attaching clips for you that contain my audio pareidolia.

Overall, this sounds to my ear most similar to a native American dialect. There's one passage, the third passage, that sounds tonal in nature, like Chinese, and even reminds me a bit of Chinese. I can hear the Native American dialect, but again is that because you suggested it...

The first passage ends and has a soft pop right after it concludes. This might be a tongue pop, possibly an actual part of the spoken language. I have recorded enough pops, clicks, smacks, huffs and grunts to be suspicious when I hear it. Especially when there are words being spoken that I cannot understand.

There's a loud knock in the middle of the first passage. Any idea what that is? Sounds like it might be from inside the shed. Lots of knocking have been noticed including building slaps.

. . .

In the second passage, there are more than just phonemes, there are clear morphemes in there. Exciting stuff, if this is not a human language. WOW!!!!!!!!!!!!!!!

Between the six and eight-second marks, I can hear a second voice speaking, farther in the distance, tonal pitch changes, very fast, and it's hard to discern what's being said. Yes, I believe that the communication stream at times seems to be faster than at first glance.

The third passage is excellent, very clear. The first morpheme almost seems to have a brassy/metallic note to it. But that might just be an artifact induced by the recording environment. I really can't say what's going on here, but there are so many morphemes and pitch changes that this is obviously some form of speech. That is the other thing, the tonality of the voice fits other locations.

The last, fainter vocal at the fourteen-second mark sounds similar to "Danke schön," German for thank you, but that's just audio pareidolia. Maybe a Wayne Newton fan.... Whoops, am I showing my age.

After the last snore, I hear a possible knock in the distance, followed by two soft "boop" "boop" type vocals, ascending in pitch. That's a fairly squatchy signal. Yup, I agree.

What did you hear when you slowed it down?
*   The words "Good to go, Yah but,"... "Pete is that You?"... "Let us, We prepare You." All three clips are attached above.*

Also, are you considering sending this to Scott Nelson? I would. I'm leaving that up to Tobe. He's really close to Ron Morehead and I'm sure Ron will get Scott involved.

• • •

End of Email.

The audio has been available online for 2.5 years and this is the last written communication I have had about it since the summer of 2020.

I received an email from Sean P. Paterson, a member of my podcast who took me up on my challenge to decipher the language. He shot me back an email that read in short but he found a transcription.

Tobe.

The audio heard while Daryl is snoring can be heard here from about 13 seconds to 30 seconds:

https://www.facebook.com/CBSSanFrancisco/videos/340179219858902/

There is a woman narrating the actions of the lion named Phil:

"...(скажи) все равно я всех отсюда выпихаю... Филя, ну машинка новая! Все, крутит руль, сел за руль уже."

"I'll (meaning the lion) squeeze everyone out of here. Phil, it's a brand-new little car! That's it, he's turning the wheel, he already got behind the wheel".

Here is a clip of the original from the Facebook page followed by the one you captured. I tried to equalize the gain.

I reached Sean and ask more about the email. It turns out all Sean did was go on Reddit and contact a Russian community thread. He suspected it sounded Russian and went with his gut. He then put my audio clip available online for them to listen to. Sean said it was weird, immediately someone came back with a response and said, "oh, I know that clip...it was a Facebook video popular over in Russia with this lion in a golf cart." Then he found the video and had it transcribed as speaking Russian. I laughed at the prospects of this all being explained so simply. Then I asked Sean, "Well how did all these military-trained language experts miss this?" He agreed that was weird. The other strange thing is how did someone's phone just turn on to a video while we were sleeping, what was the loud hit sound that's not in the video and why does the opening of the video look so much like the green metal shop we were sleeping in? The only other weird thing about it, well everything is weird about it, is the fact you never see the woman in this video actually speaking Russian. Perhaps a moot point, but it would help close the mystery woman audio a bit quicker.

Also, what about the woven cord and levitation. Those may not be connected to the audio, but it seems like an event that unfolded by the same energy. I'm frustrated with this part of the Owl Moon Lab. I guess it's possible something manipulated Darrell's phone again and the experts just made a mistake.

While writing this book and editing the photos, videos, and sounds, I felt this chapter would be the hardest to end. Darrell and I were as diligent as we could be with categorizing and reviewing all the data. However, this was not always the case. While continuing to triple-check our work, the painstaking process of labeling files stored on my external hard drive was sometimes never done. I would just store the files as quickly as possible into a folder that said, "SOUNDS" or "VIDEOS." After I found out about the possible link between the Mystery Woman sounds and the Russian tiger video, which was actually filmed at the Taigan Zoo Park in Crimea, I remembered something that seemed connected to the Owl Moon Lab. Three days after the sounds were captured, a massive mountain lion was caught on my thermal camera. I forgot all about the footage but knew it existed somewhere in the massive storage files.

After only a couple days of searching for the video, the file was found. To be clear, seeing a mountain lion in the wild out in Cottage Grove is pretty rare. Some people go their whole life and never see one. Now, who does that sound like? In this case, the mountain lion is captured on the gravel road walking from right to left past my camper.

It's filmed from a fairly close distance, about 60 feet away. The footage, shot on my thermal FLIR camera, was recorded while I slept. This would be one of those moments I would set up my thermal camera outside the bathroom rooftop vent and simply record until the battery died. The video plainly shows a very large cat meandering the road, occasionally stopping to smell the woods. You can see the large neck slope from the muscular front shoulders. The back end fits the proportions of a mountain lion with its signature long tail. We compared our size to it and guessed it to be over 6 feet in length. It was difficult for me to not see the connections between the Crimean Zoo video and now this. Both videos were shot near a green metal enclosure, both with a large cat. But what about the sounds and the language?

I began to dig one more time into the "Mystery or Crimean Zoo Lady" sounds. Like almost everything I've explained here, there's a balance and choreography to the interactions, something I call the Tailor Effect. Things that happen at a time and place for a specific reason, no matter how bizarre. What if the language was Hebrew or an offshoot from the middle east? I recall previously mentioned researcher Scott Taylor, no relation to the Tailor Effect, that mentioned his experience of Sasquatch using Aramaic to spell out words with gifted Scrabble letters. Could it be that the language experts who reviewed the audio could not translate it due to its ancient origins? After only a little bit of online digging, I found out that, indeed, the Jews migrated to Russia, including Ukraine and Crimea. They were a huge influence on the culture and were mentioned as far back as the year 1030. Specifically, the Crimean Jews are known as the Crimean Karaites, an offshoot of the Turkish and Hebrew/Aramaic Jew. Their language, commonly known as Yiddish, is a pidgin of these ancient mixed cultures. Jews from all parts of Israel, including Hebron, The Anakim, or Land of Giants, settled specifically in Crimea. Once again, the link was made between Hebron and the Owl Moon Lab. Could it be possible there was a greater symbolic meaning to my recording and the online video? If so, one could look at this in a couple of ways, I believe.

What if the Crimean zoo video is a pidgin of ancient Yiddish, and it's connected to Hebron, the land of Anakim/Giants? That alone would be an astounding bit of synchronicity, that albeit complex, makes sense to this story. Furthermore, a lion seen in both instances is totally symbolic of the Jewish faith as the Biblical symbol of God, better known as the Lion of Judah. Could it be this was not so much a warning to us while we slept that a lion is prowling the green metal shop? But a warning to a type of evil surrounding the land, that God patrols and guards this home or portal.

Since then, I've had three people tell me that audio is definitely not Russian. One of the last people to assert this was an abductee from Australia that follows my case. He said it's a draconian statement between a mother and daughter who were there on our property while we slept. These are reptilian-type beings that he knew well. He said the conversation was a deliberate message from a mother to her daughter that she should not have followed her here and she should know her place and go back that way.

I should drop this single mystery from The Lab, but I feel as though we are not done yet.

THE LION, THE LADY AND WOVEN CORD

18

APPORTS

O bjects were given to us or we were interacted with almost every day during the spring, summer and fall of 2018. As I said before, they ranged in size and scale, and some were even alive at one time. However, apportation gifts belong in their own unique category. Now to be fair, we're unsure as to how the gifts got to where they landed. At one point, Darrell found a baseball-sized rock sitting in the middle of his living room. I got a 5-inch chunk of petrified wood in my trailer sink. Unless we were sleepwalking, there was no way for us to drop these items off on our own. Plus, I think, if you're near an apportation taking place, it can make a distinct pop or snap sound. For example, one day Darrell and I were in the shop downloading audio and outside the drawn shop doors was my Jeep with the tailgate left open. I had on my headphones and noticed Darrell turn his head to the side and so I asked him "what's up?" He said, "You didn't hear that bang or pop sound?" I pointed to my headset and went back to listening to the prior evening's audio file. It's important to note I'm organized when it comes to my automobile. I make sure to vacuum it and store items in the proper space. In the back trunk area, I keep a wool blanket laid down to protect the upholstery and plastic fittings. It's just an old, olive WWII wool blanket, I think I snagged at a garage sale years ago and is always kept folded in a rectangle lying flat in the trunk. After a few minutes, we hear someone pull up in the driveway. It was an attendee to one of my live shows at the pub, who lived about a mile away and had promised to swing by and say hello. As I walked out to greet him with Darrell, I notice something new laying on the blanket. It's a small, rusted trench can opener that a soldier might use in WWII. They were issued with every dog tag back then and were very distinctive with their swiveled razor-sharp point. I yell, "No way." Darrell said, "Oh geez, what now?" I immediately roll the camera and tell Darrell to look on the blanket. He squints and walks over to what I see is a new item. The neighbor had some idea of the action at Darrell's and as a prior assistant to the late great author Lloyd Pye, was curious. We caught the neighbor up to speed while Darrell and I once again marveled at the new delivery. An Army blanket and an Army trench opener. The snap or pop sound being very curious as to perhaps a moment when it transferred through whatever quantum means into an exact spot outside our view. Again, this was not a random object placed in a random area, this was an object of comparison and significance to where it landed. We had far too many examples of this taking place and this was another. A WWII Army blanket matched with an issued Army can opener.

MILITARY CAN OPENER

I've spoken of my son's involvement with some of this tangentially, but for the most part, due to health reasons and being spooked by the things he witnessed with me, he was kept away. I was also working close to fifty hours a week on the road and unable to see him due to this factor. I stayed in touch with him on the phone while I was away at work and checked in with him with a call or text. I was heading back from Seattle one day when I was on the phone with him, and he knew about most of the weirdness at Darrell's. He would call me and ask, or I would call him and report. We were discussing all this when he said, "I thought I saw a feather on the dashboard of Mom's car the other day that did not belong to us, but it turned out it was hers." I said, "ya, that would be interesting if an object got from a-b like that." I told him that I loved him and hung up the phone while I found a rest stop.

About an hour later I was driving and I get a text from Darrell so I pull over yet again to another rest area and read it. It says, "Look what I found. Ya know that 8-foot-tall log out front I had delivered that's standing up on its end, there's a white agate sitting on the top of it." He sends me the photo and says, "I have no clue as to how that got up there." The white agate was about the size of a wedding ring with a little tiny white bubble in the middle. I tell him to take a close photo of it and maybe don't touch it till I get back. Darrell says, "I ain't gunna mess with it, I gotta take the dog to the groomer now anyway." I said, "Ok, I'm about four hours out and will see ya soon."

Within the hour I get another call from Darrell who blurted out, "It's gone, I was just looking at it an hour ago and it is gone." I said, "Darrell, you gotta let me call you right back." Out of only sure boredom from driving for hours on the interstate, I think to myself, I should check with my son...we were just talking about apports and gifts. WHAT IF, we could catch one in the act? What if we could document one in transit? I call him.

I said, "Son don't freak out, but I want you to look for something outside or inside the house." I could hear the sigh of a young man on the other end agree to help, but "What am I looking for Dad?" I said, "I want you to look for an orange stone that may be out of place around there." Now, why did I say orange instead of white? Well, I needed total confirmation he wasn't going to prank his old man. Better yet, I said, "I'll call you back on FaceTime and see you looking around the house." He agreed to call right back and video stream the search. As he rounded the corners of the house bedroom hall and into the bathroom, I see him pan down to the threshold of the floor, "What the heck is that, Dad, oh my gosh!" He zoomed in and picked up a white agate on camera. He turns it on its edge, and I see the distinct white bubble from Darrell's photo in comparison. I tell him the story and he begins to freak out with me. Then my son exclaimed, "I gotta call my mom." I said, "OK, I'll be by soon." I call Darrell back and relate the events.

AGATE APPORT

We decided the agate had apported some twenty-five miles to a person of significance. The Taylor was getting to know me and my family. The agate was put into a metal band-aid box at my son's house for a bit and periodically he would shake the box to see if it was still in there. Once he told me he shook the box and it made no sound. He put the box down to shake it again later and the familiar sound of something small and hard in an empty can bouncing around was present.

My son and his mother would go on to report other objects being moved around the outside and inside of the house, including one that seemed to catch everyone's attention when eight pumpkins were taken from the back patio during Halloween and stacked up, one on the other, atop the door. I believed the phenomena was trying to spread and enjoy new eyes for a new game.

An apportation is the mysterious cousin to a teleportation. The two interact the same way, but as where apports through space and time move an object from A to B without explanation; a teleport is theorized to move biologicals in the same way. I suspected that Darrell's whole property may be one large portal for apports and teleports. There seemed to be ample evidence for the geography to be infused with what typical spirit activity is said to be charged from. A huge deposit of gold and quartz was found in the nearby creeks and rivers. The element of flowing water and mineral deposits is long rumored to be a key location for paranormal or spirit activity. Although we never researched the details surrounding these factors, it was one thing we noted as a possibility. Also, there were at least three natural springs that flowed on or near the property. One of these springs was only 15 feet away from the Adams's property line. My camper was right beside one of these springs and only a tree and several overgrown blackberry bushes kept me from getting to it.

Once, around 12 pm in July 2018, I was moving cables from the back to the front of my camper. As I bent down to grab the cables, I felt something hit my shoulders and head. It was the unmistakable sensation of cool mist landing on me. It was like the mist you might feel briefly at the produce aisle as you're grabbing a head of lettuce, not large droplets, but a small light spray of water falling down around you. I called for Darrell to come out and feel the air in the same spot. He was amazed as I was as we stood behind the trailer and cooled down in the blazing sun. We held our arms out and felt it was only happening in one 2-foot area at the front of the trailer. I wanted to blame the AC unit or the natural spring for this occurrence, but in the end we could not debunk it.

So much of the ghost-type activity recorded on audio sounded as though something was teleporting into this realm. It would almost be like a frequency was being tuned and other times you would hear something land and then breathe, walk, moving, hitting or just plain interacting. However, most of the time you would hear nothing leave or depart. This was especially noted with occurrences in enclosed spaces that would require a physical door to be opened at the very least.

The last apport I recall concerns where I live now in the Olympic Peninsula of Washington State. When I moved up here, Darrell was still living at The Lab, and since there were so many windblown trees all around our property I took it upon myself to learn how to chainsaw carve. I carved Sasquatch faces out of cedar and was getting crafty with the design. It would have the deep sunken eyes, broad hooded nose and hair flowing from the cheeks down to the chin. I used a drill sander, map gas and black spray paint to finish it off. One day I get a call from Darrell saying he found something unusual near the shop wall. It was a small chunk of cedar with black paint and burnt edges. I said, "Darrell can you zoom up on that and take a closer pic." It was an exact match of pieces of cedar faces littered across the wood-shop. It wouldn't be the last time The Lab winked at me.

WOOD WATCHER CHUNK

19

SMOKE AND MIRRORS

E ven after all this, I was still trying to figure out a more rational explanation. From my own personal experiences with the phenomena one on one, I had to debunk a little harder. One possibility I had to consider was the possibility I was being tricked by technology or a chemical. It wasn't high electromagnetic doses, we tested the area on more than one occasion and never had a spike on our meter higher than normal. Could I have been part of a larger government or private project aware of my online presence and wanted to muddy the waters? The book Chameleo, written by author Robert Guffey, details events surrounding an individual who claims he was stalked and harassed by invisible people. Theories are explained by an engineer named Richard Schowengert as to how this might occur. Showengert, who details a full 2.5-hour interview in the book, says he helped engineer an "electro-optical camouflage" under a government project called "Project Chameleo." Furthermore, it sights an unclassified project called "The Voice of God," a type of technology that can beam voices into targeted individuals from source to skull. However, beaming experiences into your skull that did not occur and capturing on camera is another thing. Most of what we caught on camera, however, was after the fact. It was nearly impossible to catch anything on film the moment it happened without recording twenty-four seven. Had we purchased one security doorbell like RING, I could have monitored a live day and night video feed from my cell phone.

I even toyed with the idea the London Tracks were being covered up by compromising sources who would otherwise have contributed validity. I knew there was no way to prove this and to be fair, it was wrong of me to consider I was even that important. The physical evidence we gathered was good, but it hardly seemed enough to blow up a secret plan. There was nothing to go on other than what we could prove and show, if that was even important. Anytime I tried to collect data or evidence, I always tried to do this to chronicle a journal or diary. I was not always successful at that, but it was my goal to understand and remember this as it happened.

I had paranoid people in my life severely crippled by going down every rabbit hole. I could not allow myself to become them and sought wise counsel from friends and family. If I could get them to experience it, even better.

20

THE WALL

A lthough we did have communication via audio and gifts, there was also communication with four small twigs. The four small twigs would suddenly appear on the south shop wall. These sticks, or glyph sticks, were like an ordinary branch broken off into four sections. I had never been a fan of people noticing every branch in the forest being some sign of communication, and for the most part, the majority of the sticks glyphs found are forest litter. Why were these any different? Well, firstly they suddenly showed up in the gravel against the South wall. They were a specific design like one might make with a Rune alphabet. I forget exactly the first glyph left, but it was a specific shape that caught my eye. There we got most of our communication in stick forms that would change up almost every other day.

On some days we would get three twigs in a row all lined up and the fourth twigs crossing between the three horizontally. We would change the twigs around and bundle them together and leave them to see what would happen next. Then we would come back and the twigs would all be in a new glyph shape, always the same four twigs and usually a new shape. However, on a couple of occasions the shapes would repeat and what appeared as emphasis was placed near the glyph. For example, a small gift would be left near the twigs like a shiny children's toy or a small rusty screw. We decided we would continue to change the glyph twigs all the time and photograph the new shapes. We left stuff as well, either near or inside the glyph, and there again the glyph would be reformed into a new design and the object we left would be moved significantly. Sometimes the objects would be placed 20 feet away in the back of Darrell's pick-up bed or tucked under a large

stone nearby. We set out a brick near the glyph spot and left things atop that would more easily expose it on a makeshift altar, items like small shiny stones and found objects. Again, there was hardly ever an item taken but only moved or added to.

GLYPHS AND STICK SIGN

As winter approached we took all the items we had received and glued them down to a 2x4. This must have been over forty items. As we lay them down and recalled the story of each item's significance, we noticed something that was worth remarking on. The items went from small to large as the objects chronologically sat in a row; one of the first gifts being the small blue plastic dinosaur and one of the last being an old rusty arrow.

I set out these gifts, far too many to list off each story behind them, attached them to a 2x4, and placed them in the gravel next to the left of the glyph spot. It was actually directly parallel and pushed up against the metal shop wall as to provide a visual marker for us to photograph a before and after. A couple days after we left it out there, we noticed the Christmas ball, which was pristine when we found it under my oar, and which was now busted in the center. A small sliver shard of glass was glinting off it from the gravel. I referred to my before photo and noticed that the gifts were now going from left to right in the wrong order. Instead of going from small to big, they were now going from big to small. Something had picked up the 2x4 and spun it 180. In doing so it looked like they rushed the process and broke the Christmas ornament. This was accidental because we actually found shards of silver hidden under a sheet of plywood about 12 feet away. It reminded me of moments I would try and hide a mistake from my mother before she got home. We left the gift board out for a week or two after that and a few more items would appear directly on the board.

On another occasion, I left out a hidden object under a pile of gravel near the glyph spot. It was a bright red plastic Silly Putty egg. I made sure not to open it and leave the putty as the factory had sealed it. Once buried under a couple inches of piled gravel, I took a photo and filed the moment away like we had done so often before. A couple weeks later Darrell, Ren the neighbor and I had a couple of beers and caught up. I asked Darrell had he noticed the gravel exposed yet where the egg was, and he said no. I went over and checked with my before photo. It looked like Darrel said, untouched. Every small chunk of gravel was in the exact same position as the before photo, nothing was moved. I peeked just the same at the spot and pushed back the stones to reveal the egg "eggxatly" where I left it. However, something was different, there was a small dusty fingerprint on the edge of the egg. I recall wearing blue rubber gloves when I buried it and wiping it down. I guess I could have missed a spot and it was my print, but I called the boys over just the same. I handed the egg to Darrell and told him to look at the fingerprints. I then asked Darrell to open it and I will record. So as I rolled the video, he cracked the egg open to reveal a small silver bead halfway into the putty. It was about half the size of a grain of rice with two holes on the side like any bead would need. Off to the side of the putty was a small dermal fingerprint that showed what could only be a human type of fingerprint. Someone had left this; it was not an oversight. The gravel rocks, for one, had never moved and were exactly as I had left them.

SILLY PUTTY EGG AND JEWELS

After I had moved back up the road I would still come down and check on the south wall and the gifts. I decided a thank you was in order and took note from a story investigator Scott Taylor had told me about. He said he was working with an EESI up in Washington State using Scrabble pieces to communicate with them. He would spell something out and leave spare letters. Within days there would be a spelled-out response and it was in line with answering the previous statement. Sometimes the spelled-out words would be in a different language but still transcribable. One language was Aramaic, an old Hebrew language that dates back before Christ.

I left out my own version and make it a little more interesting. The small silver bead left inside the silly putty egg and perhaps the gravel pieces show an extreme use of careful placement. I found the tiniest small wooden squares I could at a garage sale and made my own Scrabble letters on them. The small wooden blocks were as small as a pencil eraser and on each side of every cube I wrote all the letters in the alphabet two times. I then used the remainder of the small blocks to write numerical signatures 0-9. I then grabbed a flat stone near the glyph spot and spelled out, "Thank You for Gifts." The remainder of the unused blocks I left in a plastic spray paint lid and placed up against the metal wall. My hope was that something would say something in return or leave something of significance near the flat stone. After I'd been out of town for about a week, I asked Darrell if he'd checked the flat stone for any movement. He said he had not but would now. I waited by the phone and he messaged me a photo. I still get chills when I think of this moment and aside from all the other moments I've mentioned, this one is up there. Spelled out below my statement in small wood blocks was the simple phrase "W3L4ME." It was all in order from left to right under the blocks I had laid out and the plastic spray paint lid was not tipped over. I took it to possibly mean WELCOME and the numbers used made perfect sense. I had not made enough letters for whoever did this to use the letters E and C. Instead, they used the closest shape they could find numerically to fit into the correct area.

SPELLING ROCK OR OUIJA BOARD

In translation it was perhaps supposed to look as close to the letters used to say an appropriate response, "W=E/3=L=C/4=M+E. Of course, the O or Zero was not there, but it was still intriguing that the blocks were delicately taken out of a precarious plastic lid and placed below a statement. This was a breakthrough, but a bittersweet one at that. Just days before I devised this plan, I came back to check the property and out on the front lawn I saw a For Sale sign. It would be the second time Darrell had sought to sell the property. It had been only fourteen months since they bought it, but the housing market was too good not to capitalize on. It wasn't long before this moment that the house would sell to a couple from Beverly Hills. Darrell let me know they had only a couple of months before closing and the house would change hands. I think it's important to note the sale of the property had nothing to do with the activity that was present. I tried as hard as I could to gather interest before it actually sold to strangers, but nobody would bite. What the hell do you advertise anyway when it comes time to advertise a home like this? For Sale, "Spacious ranch style portal with 3 bedrooms and 2 baths. Teleports and levitation likely from quaint front and backyard. Scenic view of the Umpqua Mountain Range where daily visits from Sasquatch, UFOs and ghosts are an added bonus of an active Portal. A trained real estate agent, I was not.

21

THE OWL MOON WILD

May 2019 - Port Orchard, Washington

I arrived at the long dirt road heading down to Eryn's cabin. In tow was my 16-foot trailer and everything I owned. It was a much needed move and Eryn and I were in love. The 5.5-hour commute or daily phone calls were not enough. It had been two years of long-distance devotion and we needed some clarity. It was a tough decision, being a state away from my son, but he was freshly seventeen years old, and I would still see him every first of the month.

Eryn was a Washington native and had grown up only about twenty miles away on a beautiful island in the Puget Sound. She'd been all over the world and had lived many lives. I felt I had, but not to the extent she had. Moving into her cabin nestled deep in the woods was an extreme makeover. The isolation of being surrounded by tall Cedars and Doug Firs in our postcard cabin was all I could have ever dreamed of. We built a life together and started fresh under the spell of the PNW summer.

A couple of months before I arrived, there was a texted photo sent from Eryn. It was taken from the front porch and focused on the wooden beams that supported the a-frame rooftop. The text read "these are new...what the fuck?" On the beams were small chalky white handprints wrapped around the wood beams at different heights. They showed up overnight, as far as Eryn could tell, and matched no known hands from her or her family. She has a twenty-year-old son, but his hands are much larger than these. This would be the first sign there was more than synchronicity going on related to the Owl Moon Lab. The handprints we documented and collected in Darrell's guest bedroom were smaller than these, but they had the same chalky white stain-infused imprint. Both were found near or on a doorway or threshold. In the case of Eryn's find, they were on the outside of the house, which at least helped with any concern of someone sneaking inside. I could tell Eryn was not pleased with the possibility of something acknowledging my move, but what were we to do. I spent a couple of days studying the differences. The prints in Washington were about thirty percent larger than the OML prints. The fingers were longer and more human looking. They did not gnarl or curl inwards and instead extended out straight as they wrapped around the corner of every beam in front of the cabin. Some handprints were as low as 3 feet from the bottom of the porch and others were eye level with me about 5-6 feet off the porch. I didn't collect them even though I was tempted. I wanted Eryn to know I did not come with ulterior motives of studying a potential new portal. However, she was keeping a very detailed journal of everything happening and it was a lot. I had no idea what I was about to bump into living there and The Tailor phenomena wasn't going anyplace.

CHALKY WHITE HANDLED BEAMS

As the summer approached, my monthly trips down to Oregon would consist of me taking my son out for lunch or dinner, a movie and then catching up with my mother and her husband. I was always invited down to Darrell and Cindy's before the property sold but would have to camp in my Jeep or sleep outside. If I was coming down to see family, I might as well soak up the last little bits of the OML before it sold.

The first two months of visitations I decided to journal just how activity would react to me burying things on all four corners of the property. I grabbed a couple of thunder eggs, agates and a garden spade. I then dug about 6-8 inches down into the soil, dropping the stones like seeds. Instead of covering them up, I grabbed flat rocks like tombstones and placed them over the hole. They did not stick out at all, and you would miss them if you didn't watch me leave them there.

The first month, I didn't even mention I was digging this. It was my final attempt at reconfirming whatever was happening was tapping into something unexplainable by ordinary means. Thirty days after I left the four hidden holes I would come back to see the stone had been slid off the hole and the thunder egg or agate had been placed near it. On one occasion, the agate had been taken while I was asleep in my lawn chair by the fire pit and placed in the back of Darrell's pick-up.

I would continue to record when I was down there and so did Darrell. The sounds were just as they were before. The shop was just as active as ever and most nights when I would sleep out there it was almost impossible to get a full night of rest. Sleep was always in rare supply when you were trying to study it. I would balance my nights with a couple of Keystone Lights and a thermos of Coffee. At this point, I'd seen far too little for the amount of physical evidence we'd amassed. I wanted to see who was responsible for this, if not to just hear them, and only see what had taken place after they left. I had to know for certain, Sasquatch or something else, one way or another.

About a week before Darrell and Cindy were closing and leaving the keys to another owner, I had one final stay. I backed in my Jeep that evening and sprawled out my lawn chair and recording equipment. The cold air was coming in the evening now and the fog blanketed down across the valley. I stayed up for as long as I could watching the stars and listening through my portable speaker for more ghostly EVPs. I had two days left before I had to leave, and this would be the last access I had to the land before the Adams moved. I lay there waiting to come in and out of sleep when sounds would erupt in the shop. Huddled under my blanket at around 3:30 am I awoke to go pee and noticed the portable speaker had turned off. I fumbled for the power button as I nested under my wool blanket. The fire I'd made in the fire pit was out as well. As I turned on my speaker, it made its usual loud powering up tone. Immediately, I heard something in front scatter the gravel and shift its weight. I slowly pulled back my blanket and peeked out into the moonless night sky. Nothing. I let my eyes adjust as I lay there, slowly bending my chair out of the recumbent position. I saw something behind the front passenger side of my Jeep about 25 feet in front of me. It was a long set of light-colored feet resting on the dark gravel road. They were carefully pulling away from my view as I watched them aim back towards the gravel road. Then in a shot, they bolted and fled. As they ran there was only one simple crunch on the long gravel road that extended at least 40 feet to the tree line filled with brambles and dried leaves. No other sound was heard to give any indication something was running away. The only other sound I heard immediately after that initial crunch was a vocal I will never forget. It was like a scream and yell all at once. Within moments of that sound, I could hear above me in the trees a second similar sound either answering back or it was the same individual traveling around a mile in under thirty seconds. I got up and ran to the area with no flashlight. I wanted to meet whoever it was on mutual terms. I walked down the road about 100 yards and saw and heard nothing. I went to grab my recorder to listen for the vocal I just heard, but it was not impressive. I don't really know how that was possible, it just fell short of the usual quality of vocals we captured.

I stayed awake till morning and related the events to Darrell. We both went looking for tracks in the gravel and saw only a couple of scuff marks. It was all I saw that moved me close to the truth and for me it was almost enough to say for certain.

Right before Darrell and Cindy moved, Darrell sent me photos of the south side of the shop, deep in the gravel where barefooted tracks were embedded past the gravel layer. They showed a size-15 five-toed track right and left foot. I drove down a couple days after and examined the prints. They showed the deep impaction of gravel settled down into and beyond the ground layer. We tried to duplicate it by stomping our boots as hard as we could but there was no way to compare. In my opinion it would have taken something much larger than a size-15 foot to pull that off through mere inertia. The only way it could have been done was to be faked or for something to vibrate the rocks down into the earth as it stood there. It happened a couple days later near the shovel and rake we used to test study the area, only this time you could see the individual toes separate the rocks as it dug down deep in the gravel. It would be foolish of me not to at least consider it was a farewell move from a Sasquatch. I no longer had the luxury of disbelief.

GRAVEL TRACKS

It looked to be the final nod from what we had called the Owl Moon Lab. The house sold to a couple from California. The husband was a science fiction fan and was considering turning one of the grades into a private science fiction library. They were informed of the rich history of the house and until the Fall of 2019, there has been little contact with them on their observations of the property.

I was overall very envious of their purchase and often wonder what more could have been learned there if I could study it, acknowledge it, and get to know it even better. Skinwalker Ranch had the kitchen sink effect to study it, but we had limited resources for a short amount of time.

During the winter of 2019/20, Darrell decided he would go for a hike behind his old property in search of signs or what he calls stick structures. They've been found before in that area and so it wasn't too long before Darrell found massive barefooted tracks heading in from his old house up to the top of the ridge. This would lead to an eventual sighting nearby. He called me the same afternoon he said he watched from his truck a tall, lanky upright figure running down the power lines. It was running so fast you could barely follow it with your eyes. He squeezed off a photo just before it jumped into some blackberry bushes, but all you see is at most a blurry shadow. A couple days later he would walk down in the area with the neighbor Ren. There was little to no sign for them to track and they had no interactions with the figure spotted.

A month or 2 after that, Darrell would go back into the woods with Ren where he felt like the phenomenon was coming in from. There were loads of examples of audio and video where strange lights in the sky were directly around or near the forested power lines. He decided somewhere between this area and the creek was the best place to explore. It was in this area, a place he called The Owl Moon Wild, where the strangeness occurred regularly.

Ren and Darrell found a spot on Google Maps where an old logging landing was accessible. It was just above his old land hidden in the woods. The grown-over area was just big enough to drive a couple of pick-up trucks down before waiting for night to fall. So that's what he and Ren did. One evening, as they were waiting for dusk, Darrell and Ren both saw lights appear in the woods. They described them as typical balls of light that would occasionally flash. They knew how deep the incline was for the light to appear in the thorny forest. The lights were elevated over a natural human's height and ability. They watched as the lights seemed to come closer, appear and disappear. This was Ren's first true encounter with these lights we had been telling him about in 2018. Soon the lights would dim out and the darkness would fill with a terrible stench in the air. This wretched death smell was mixed with the unmistakable sound of bi-pedal footsteps all around them. They watched the tree line and nervously waited for the woods to reveal the source of this. It would become too much for both to handle and they decided it best to leave while they still had options to do so on this one-lane road.

That evening, after Darrell got home and parted ways with Ren, he messaged me about the strange events. Upon powering on his phone and reviewing some photos with me online, he noticed something off. There was a video on his camera roll. It was just a black screen with around 15-20 seconds of audio. It had no time or date stamp associated with it. Darrell reviewed the weird black video and immediately heard what is plain to hear. The video starts off with someone chewing something very crunchy. While this is happening, you hear what sounds like Darrell's exact voice speaking in an unknown language.

The voice erupts in a very strange electronic burst. "Eeehchoo-lauww." Then the crunchy chewing stops along with whatever is sounding like Darrell's voice. Then a third sound comes into play, a synthesized voice of an unknown woman. She says, "Now what's gunna happen when they get out here?" Then back again comes the crunchy chewing and whatever is using Darrell's voice to say this last statement, "Thaaaey-may-muh-sssuhhh!" It ends with the mystifying crunchy chewing sound.

PHONE HIJACK AND HIJYNX

It isn't uncommon for EESIs to report strange electronic anomalies to their phone. Images or photos of things they have never seen or taken pictures of suddenly turn up on people's devices. It's like something is seeing something from around their property and then mentally inserts it onto their phone.

Lisa Phay showed me her own digital hijack. On more than one occasion she would have photos turn up on her smartphone camera roll. Somehow and someway there would be extreme close-ups of goats eyes, as though something borrowed her phone while she was asleep and ran up to a nearby goat before shoving the lens right up to its eyes for a photo.

The Owl Moon Wild, although not the Lab, was abundantly active for Darrell during 2019-20. When I could, I would balance out work and family by heading down from Washington to Oregon and staying in the proximity of my old stomping grounds. The main area of the Owl Moon Wild was easily accessible off an old logging road. Darrell would still visit the area about once a week and find intricate weavings done mainly to Maple branches. The sticks would be braided in twisted loops. Some of these sticks would be braided to other Maple tree branches or twigs and pulled at the base of the trees. I had never seen this before in person, so when he showed me, I saw the intricate beauty of design and art associated with it. I couldn't help but think of the human behavior associated with creating baskets or even braiding hair. It could have been done with a human hand but given the strength it took to bend and ark some of the larger fresh branches and twist them in tight braids, I thought not. It seemed like typical and reliable Sasquatch weavings.

DELICATE WEAVES

Although my new home in Washington was six hours north, I felt once again drawn back to the mystery of this land. In every way it was relentless with its powerful unsolvable puzzle. My new home was everything I could have dreamt of, as far as Eryn and our house went, but it was not the Owl Moon area. I tried to push back my urge to drive down to Oregon every month for a couple of days, but I was unsuccessful. It helped to have family nearby, including my son, but I was overpowered and seduced by the land. I felt as though I was so close to something concrete that I could see and perhaps even know, a dream-like state that would be my hidden and privileged reality. These private thoughts eventually bubble to the surface and it's best to be honest with where your head is at. I told Eryn I felt as though I had to continue my visits and I had no choice. I needed to be understood as someone who was compelled to continue. I could see she was worried about my drive and focus mainly on this mystery that would never give itself up. At one point I recall saying to her, "The land is my family, I feel as though I've left a human relationship behind, like a lover." The look on her face was one of disgust and I can't say I blame her. Of course, I immediately regretted saying it. I would, however, travel down to the land and check on it as often as our relationship would allow.

These unnatural urges by the paranormal to beacon a man's interest are written about throughout history. Look to Greek mythology and the call of the Sirens. Of course, the ploy of the Sirens call is to pull and steer unwitting sailors to dangerous reefs and rocks. A sort of ancient Screwtape I spoke of earlier.

Darrell would continue to message news about interactions in the wild. He was beginning to take steps with new researchers using familiar techniques of study. Included in that were feeding stations and cameras. I was against these methods while living down there and sometimes I thought both moves were disrespectful to the overall cunning of Sasquatch and whatever was around them. However, this is what Eryn said, "Not my circus and not my monkey!" So I withdrew my opinion and mainly just visited as the site was set up when I got there.

The first thing I noticed that was different was the use of food to interact. Mainly, Darrell would use peanut butter as a type of tree slather. He would take huge jars of cheap creamy peanut butter and paint the bark of Doug fir trees with it. In some cases, using a spatula to slide the creamy goo up as high as 7 feet. Then he would take the remainder of the peanut butter and some smaller unopened peanut butter jars and hide them under stumps. Pointed at these trees and stumps would be one or two game cameras. After a couple days, Darrell would either find the peanut butter was taken clean off the trees or the lids unscrewed from the ones on the stump. The cameras would never reveal the source of how this was done and often showed strange pixilation beside the tree that looked like a heat wave or mirage sliding up near the food, and then in the next frame there'd be nothing.

Although the contents may be empty and there was little to show on film, there were signs of visitations. Chief amongst these signs were the deep footprints we would find heading into these areas. The footprints would come up the ridge only when near the food, as though whatever left them, came up from the deep ravine below using stealth. There was little to no sign or tracks available to study, only the occasional long white branch stacked in a row on the ground or up against a tree. Yet, when the tracks were found near the food, they were hard to miss. As large as some of them were, the immense depth caught us off guard. What most people don't know about impressions in the forest is how hard it is to impress at all. The resilient and spongey substrate was comprised of tree roots, limbs, stone and leaf litter. The earth does not even start until you dig beyond these elements. So, when walking, stomping or jumping on the dense spongey forest floor the ground acts more like a bouncy cushion, rather than surface that takes the shape of a foot. This fact is increased more so with size. The larger the foot, the fewer lbs per inch to reach a depth. Think of a ski pole hitting the snowpack compared to a snowshoe. Less depth on overall size.

So, when we saw the tracks, we knew what kind of size we had to be talking about. The foot was on average 14.5-17 inches long with a step length of 6-8 feet. The depth was anywhere between 2-4 inches at a 90-degree angle from the heel all the way to the toes. We tried to duplicate my size 12-inch boot on video but we didn't even come close. There was absolutely no way these tracks were made by stomping or digging them into existence. The dirt was collected around the base of the track heel and compressed. We would measure the tracks, video and cast them. On a couple of occasions, we would invite family and friends to join us for the excursion.

OWL MOON WILD TRACKS

22

IMPOSING PHYSICIANS

Washington was getting under my skin more, and my new home life with Eryn was becoming something normal instead of a novelty. We would spend the evenings watching the stars over the outdoor fire pit or looking for new places to beach comb. Inevitably the world of Sasquatch was all around us living in the woods. It was impossible to ignore the PNW culture that embraces the native mythos. I kept the Strange Bräu Radio podcast in full production weekly. Eventually, I even found a place in Port Townsend that would grant me space to do a monthly live show. Enter the historically haunted Manresa Castle. It was in the Castle I could build another audience who would attend or be interviewed about their own strange encounters. It was while I was editing an episode for a live show at the Castle when I received an urgent message from Darrell that something major had happened down in Oregon.

The message read something like, "I took Mark Parker, a new researcher, witness and seasoned bow hunter down to the spot. He's been setting up there a while, leaving his game camera out and getting weird photos. Well, tonight we both went back as the sun was setting and Mark brought along his thermal monocular scope. We sat in the dark on the old road looking down the draw. As we scanned the tall tree line, we suddenly see lights flashing and hovering way off the forest floor. Maybe 50 feet or higher, but close. Then Mark and I see an orange-red one. I turn to Mark and tell him what you tell me, that colors may mean we're in for some serious shit now. It was then Mark scanned the woods to the right where he says he saw a 10-foot-tall Sasquatch coming right at us. It's super close and closing the gap. Next thing I know he runs inside the pick-up truck, and we leave in a hurry!"

Well, I immediately call Darrell and Mark, who I'd never spoken with at length. He was only a couple hours fresh from this incident when we spoke on the phone. I could hear it in his voice that the incident was traumatic and fresh. I balance my tone with him as though it were me trying to wrap my own brain around the impossible blunt confrontation of the supernatural. After about fifteen minutes of hearing on speakerphone his car throttling down the highway, I ask if we could record an interview the next day. Fortunately, he agreed to the terms, and you can listen to the full interview on Strange Bräu Radio Episode 70.

MARK PARKER INTERVIEW

Mark would not be the last person who would encounter The Owl Moon Wild. Darrell would take a handful of new researchers who were dying for an experience like we were describing. Some, if not most, were skeptical of the claims around the area, but eventually almost all had their own private proof that land did not care about personal doubt. There was no predicting when or how it would deliver on its ability to show you were not alone, but eventually if you hung around long enough the inevitable visit would happen.

Feb.14th Valentine's Day 2020

I was busy working up in Seattle as an Uber Driver and balancing the podcast with my new hobby as a part-time chainsaw carver. Eryn and I took a few days off from our hustle and drive up to see the sights in Bellingham, Washington. We booked a hotel and visited with some close friends for the evening. The next day I woke with terrible stomach pains, fever, nausea, red-eye and spontaneous visits to the toilet. What a Valentine's Day gift for her to witness. What I didn't know was how severe and transmissible these symptoms could have been.

There was just a little news around the city of some virus spreading from Wuhan, China. They called the illness Corona, and it was contagious. The word pandemic was not in full circulation yet and I was not worried about it, nor were the millions of Americans still moving about freely. After my second full day of lying in bed, wondering if I should go to the hospital for the first time in my life, I considered my symptoms to be rare and new. Could I have this Corona shit and what should I do? I never called a physician because after a few days my symptoms were gone.

You know the rest of the story regarding the shit show that was 2020, but you don't know this. Until this book, I have only mentioned this once before online and to close friends who understand that strange miracles can occur.

Around April 2020, I took a solo trip to the Owl Moon Wild. It was eerie that month driving six hours with little to no cars on the highway through Tacoma, Olympia, Portland or Salem. Every zombie apocalypse movie ran through my head as I crossed potential quarantine zone highway signs. The only people near the major roads were thousands of homeless growing in numbers as the disease raged on.

By the time I reached Cottage Grove and the turn off to The Wild, it felt like I'd just made history as the only man outside living an ordinary life. I knew Corona, or as they were now calling it, Covid-19 was a game-changer. It was dangerous, given the stats and my own possible run-in with it. So when I turned off the ignition of my Jeep and hopped out of the car, I stepped onto the familiar logging road with purpose. I looked out over the ravine and heard only the sound of a couple birds way off in the distance. The usual vacuum of sound was present once again in the dense re-prod of the forest. I spoke allowed to the trees as though they were more. As though I had learned something all these years that the forest listens and responds to those it wants to. If that was Sasquatch, ghost, aliens, fairies or whatever, I didn't care anymore about how it sounded. I knew there was something there I could not see watching me and scanning my intent. This indigenous land spirit and companion knew why I'd come, so when I spoke aloud it was for me…not for them.

I shouted, "We are in trouble! I think you know that, and this has happened before. We are not like you in so many ways, but I think we are like you in a way that you can help. We get sick and there is a great need for us to get a cure. I came to you to ask for help to treat this disease. I want you to give me a cure for Corona. I think it's time we meet, so if you are here with me now, let's finally do it. You know I am not armed, and I have no camera. I only want help and want to meet you."

Then I walked down the old deer trail that Darrell had helped wear down. The times I had been before I'd grown familiar with a large mossy Fir stump. It was hidden by a knoll behind recent twisted limbs THEY had done. It was at this stump I grabbed the old spelling blocks and spelled out WE NEED A CURE / CAN WE MEET. I left a few other gems and stones including an old sandstone fossil near the words and then simply leave. No recorder, no food and no extra letters for a response.

I drove the six strange hours directly back to Port Orchard and kind of forgot about the trip. The news cycle was all anyone was watching and if you could hustle off to the grocery store and find TP or ammo, you focused on that.

About a week later I get a message from Darrell, who knew I went down there but was unaware of why. He sends me back a photo of the stump and the words spelled out. The words were knocked around and some things were moved about, from what memory served. As he scanned up on the video, he's heard saying, "There's something black and slimy sitting here, it looks like black old slime." I texted him back and asked him to zoom in his camera if on site and he did. I could see what he was talking about. He goes on to narrate a new small video to me, "It's just sitting on this sandstone rock you left here." I have utterly no idea what this is and tell Darrell I will be down in a week, could he save it for me. He reluctantly agreed to bag and tag the weird black thing for my next trip down.

I make it down to Darrell's new house and bullshit with him in his garage. We talk about the newest activity in the woods and look over his new collection of giant plaster casts he's secured with some new researchers he took to the area. Along with these size 16s was a new batch of maple twig weaves he had snipped off and a vanity mirror he had hung with a greasy fingerprint attached to it. Amazing finds generally, but I wanted to see this weird black thing. He grabs it off the shelf and says, "It's way smaller now because it dried and shriveled up." It was roughly about half the size it was in the video and looked like a piece of ginseng to me. We thought about what it could be and even handled it for a bit seeing if the texture would ring a bell. We compared the two forms it was in, the larger black wet form and the now tiny, dehydrated form. I started to wonder if we could identify it as a natural plant that maybe fell from a tree. Perhaps a lichen or moss? Maybe even a loaded frog egg sack. We went through all the possibilities and landed on it matching one thing local to the decaying logs of the PNW. A fungus called *Exedia Glandulosa* / aka: Black Witches Butter. After reading more about this fungus, I was astounded by its herbal remedy uses that include treatment for upper respiratory infection. Could this be an answer to my request, WE NEED A CURE. Was this a cure or treatment for Covid-19? I researched more regarding its ancient uses throughout history, one hard to ignore...given my second question to the woods, CAN WE MEET? It turns out Black Witches Butter is also a psychoactive agent known to alter the conscious mind to meet the land spirits. I immediately called up a local mycologist at a Chinese Herbal store and asked them to review the photos of the suspected fungus. They agreed that it appeared to be Black Witches Butter. I told Darrell it looked to be a match and a direct answer to the request he had no idea I'd made. Then there was silence. My thoughts steered towards the obvious, what the hell do I do now? Nobody will believe this story and certainly not anyone outside the small exclusive EESI club.

I told Eryn about my findings, and I could tell she thought it was a long shot and probably just a weird coincidence. Perhaps it wasn't even a fungus, but just debris that blew its way down off a branch and landed randomly on a rock. Well, I couldn't fully disagree, and it was comforting to have someone you trust remind you that the Earth is still round. My only problem was that conclusion had a dead end. It left no room for exploration, for looking further down the rabbit hole of "what if." So, I decided to make note of it in a simple Facebook post. I wrote down what you just read and decided to weed out the weirdos like me from those that could not imagine a world where this may be possible. It was because of that post I received an email from a new friend who I'd met only briefly during a weekend Sasquatch campout. Ashlea Stinnett was, from what I could glean, a student of the mysteries and most likely an EESI herself. She seemed well educated and informed on all these familiar strange topics. I would guess my observations were correct given what she wrote. Her abbreviated message to me told tales about how she read my post on Black Witches Butter and Covid. She said it didn't sit on blinded eyes and she acted. She said she had a friend who early on was showing symptoms. She told her friend about the possible use of fungus to treat upper respiratory illness and infection. It was Ashley who suggested her friend seek a Chinese herbalist who carried strains of dried *Exedia Glandulosa*. Within twenty-four hours of taking a tincture of the Black Witches Butter, Ashlea's once ill friend had a dramatic recovery. This was amazing to learn, but I had to be careful with how I share this news. It seemed treatments and pharmaceuticals for Covid-19 were becoming ever more politicized and less about effectiveness. In fact, a growing number of friends and family on social media were getting blocked and banned altogether from familiar websites for even sharing posts that countered the World Health Organization narrative. So, I pussed out and left it alone. In fact, the little zip-lock bag with the dried sample still sits in a drawer with all the other inexplicable items from that time. Perhaps a scientist or mycologist already knows an herbal treatment such as Black Witches Butter can be used to lessen the symptoms of Covid-19, but it sure was never proven or advertised. Not to mention the aftereffects of taking this common fungus as a mind-altering substance that guides you to forest spirits.

I must write that I DO NOT suggest ANYONE follow up on this possible scientific breakthrough for Covid-19. This is not a medical suggestion, and I am not a physician. As far as how I will continue forward with a theory on it all, well I don't know. The pandemic is waning down as I write this, and vaccines are viewed as a catch-all for curing the current strain. However, if Sasquatch was the source for delivering Black Witches Butter as a treatment to the global infection, I owe them much gratitude. The whole world does.

BLACK WITCHES BUTTER

Since that time, the forest has taken on a new responsibility. These moments changed my worldview and sphere of influence forever. It was more than taking the Red Pill and simply riding a wild ride of magic and mystery, it was a change to my very DNA. My conscious and subconscious mind grew anew at The Owl Moon Lab/Wild. As it was happening, I knew it was, I could feel each moment elevating and expanding my faith in the supernatural. It was a time where religion was superseded by GOD, or GOD Source. In seeing and living in this world and viewing the cryptic Fingerprints of GOD's, it was my experience that their world is rather neutral and filled with grey areas. I can say that on the land, we never experienced evil at all. Perhaps some would view the rabbit and snake as murder for the sake of murder, but I can't. Maybe that's a mistake I will realize in the coming years. These beings or energetic forces recon with any human but seem to target individuals who may be marked from birth. I don't think I am one of those people, but Darrell was and is. I think he accesses this world as a lighthouse guides ships in the night. They seek him out like all the rest of the EESIs I've met throughout these last sixteen years.

Darrell and Cindy lived a rather ordinary life until they were led to a small homestead in the Umpqua Forest. As Darrell would often say, "I was normal until I got here." But his new normal had a price. That being, the hidden knowledge not easily shared. He could never go back to thinking Sasquatch was just a damn dirty ape. Nobody who visited the land and stayed long enough to experience the power of it could.

The Owl Moon Lab isn't unique, and we weren't special. We just noticed things, and asked, "What goes around the bend?" As strange as all this was, it seemed natural and familiar to live alongside THEM or IT. A place for a time where I lived in a paranormal experiment.

23

THE OWL MOON ALTAR

Bob struggled to find the light switch on the nearby wall. He swiped his hand back and forth behind him trying not to awaken his familiar and severe lower back pain. His gnarled and stained fingertips, brown and yellow from years of rolling his own cigarettes, finally flick the wall light on into the hallway. He pulls himself up from the couch and moans as the two dogs passed out in the kitchen, half mass their eyes his way. "Koko, Gunny…let's go," Bob grumbles. The two old farm dogs both raised their twin crippled left ears, a genetic trait left between these two elderly sibling dogs.

Bob passes by the kitchen counter, sweeping his feet past the usual dropped Pepsi cans. It used to be Jack Daniel bottles, but Vicodin didn't mix so well. Koko and Gunny follow Bob as he cracks the back sliding glass door. The usual 7:00 am morning piss n' poop was needed and both mutts were accustomed to the tradition at this time. Bob watches from the dusty and mud-pawed sliding glass door as the two dogs howl and bark as they aim straight to their usual tall grassy dumping ground.

The October breeze was cold on Bob's exposed chest. He stood in stained and ripped red sweatpants, scanning the sky to see if snow was still coming. The house was cold as well and it was, unfortunately, time to haul in another back-breaking 25 lb bag of stove pellets. Bob cracks the door open fully and when he steps out onto the covered deck, he treads on something unfamiliar. He lifts up his foot to find something halfway adhered to the bottom of his black-bottomed feet. Bob arches his foot against the rail of the sliding door and picks the substance off it. "What the hell is this?" Bob mutters, as he looks down to inspect. It was a long fresh stock of field grass, actually, it was two stocks of field grass. Bob bends over, picks up the plant and sees it's knotted in the center as though it has been tied and looped. Even stranger, in the center tied knot of the field grass, there appeared to be saliva or spit. Between the knotted strands of field grass lay two decapitated white tail rabbits, their fresh corpses resting side by. Bob kicks the bodies and sees a small amount of fresh blood pool down on the patio. He calls out "Koko, Gunny…COME!" The dogs ignore him as usual and bark incessantly at the forest edge that surrounded his double-wide. Bob yelled louder, "Get over here, you two, COME!" Both dogs turn to the source of the commanding gruff tone and take one final sniff in the lingering air. Bob quickly closes the sliding glass door and disappears inside his disheveled existence.

This was related to Eryn when she went up to help Bob move his outdoor rancid trash can. Eryn knew that Bob was aware of more than he was saying about his own personal experiences but left it. She knew the land connecting our homes was filled with ancient magic and beings. She rarely calls it Sasquatch or ghost, but instead calls them Huldufølk: meaning *the hidden people*, or elves. A new term I would try to refer to the phenomena as, but I still had my questions.

Eryn could be found during significant celestial events tending to our five acres of field and forest. There upon the Fir stumps, just like I'd done at the Owl Moon Wild, she would leave trinkets, jewels and gifts as gestures to the Huldafølk, or land spirits. It was on these moss-covered stumps The Owl Moon Altar got its name, each stump, presiding over a temple of old growth like an ancient altar. We would walk our private trails to these altars and occasionally find new items added or taken away. Eventually, I would leave my recorder atop them and find the familiar knock, hit or slap sound nearby, accompanied by a distant solitary howl or scream. Once I would even hear something jump from out of a tree and run past my recorder on two feet.

OWL MOON ALTAR SOUNDS

So far, the interaction between the new place I call home is different from what I experienced at the Lab. If I summed up the differences between the two worlds, the old world was masculine and the new world feminine. Both unique with a familiar power, but each playing to a different audience. One must know how to read a room, after all.

For the Extended Experiencers of Sasquatch Interaction and to those who seek and find a treasured power spot, your story helped me tell my own. It led me deeper and reminded me that it all not only meant something, but... it meant something else.

INTERVIEW WITH THE ADAMS

COMING SOON

To watch more archived interviews and footage about THE OWL MOON LAB
| A Paranormal Experiment

COMING SOON:

FLASH OF BEAUTY

&

NOW PLAYING ON YOUTUBE:

ALIEN BIGFOOT CONNECTION REVEALED

Made in the USA
Coppell, TX
12 December 2022

89042553R00095